Compliments of

Boston University
Executive Development Roundtable

P9-DFT-902

With best wishes,
Barry Oshry

Seeing Systems

Unlocking the Mysteries of Organizational Life

Seeing Systems

Unlocking the Mysteries of Organizational Life

■

by Barry Oshry

Berrett-Koehler Publishers
San Francisco

Berrett-Koehler Publishers, Inc.
155 Montgomery Street
San Francisco, CA 94104-4109
Tel: (415) 288-0260 Fax: (415) 362-2512

ORDERING INFORMATION

Individual sales. Berrett-Koehler publications are available through most bookstores. They can also be ordered direct from Berrett-Koehler at the address above.

Quantity sales. Special discounts are available on quantity purchases by corporations, associations, and others. For details, contact the "Special Sales Department" at the Berrett-Koehler address above.

Orders for college textbook/course adoption use. Please contact Berrett-Koehler Publishers at the address above.

Orders by U.S. trade bookstores and wholesalers. Please contact Publishers Group West, 4065 Hollis Street, Box 8843, Emeryville, CA 94662. Tel: (510) 658-3453; 1-800-788-3123. Fax: (510) 658-1834

Printed in the United States of America

 Printed on acid-free and recycled paper that is composed of 85% recovered fiber, including 15% post consumer waste..

Library of Congress Cataloging-in-Publication Data

Seeing systems: unlocking the mysteries of organizational life/by Barry Oshry.
    p. cm.

    Includes bibliographical references.
    ISBN 1-881052-73-7 (alk. paper)
    1. Social systems.   2. Organizational behavior.   3. Mangement.   I. Title.
HM131.082 1995   95-33582
302.35--dc20   CIP

First Edition
  99 98 97 96 95   10 9 8 7 6 5 4 3 2 1

For Karen

Contents

Act III Seeing Patterns of Process

Prologue: Overcoming System Blindness

We humans spend our lives in systems:
in the family,
the classroom,
the friendship group,
the team,
the organization,
the task force,
the church,
the community,
the bowling league,
the nation,
the ethnic group.
We find joy
and sadness,
exhilaration
and despair,
good relationships
and bad ones,
opportunities
and frustrations.
So much happens to us in system life,
yet system life remains a mystery.
There is so much we don't see.

When We Don't See Systems

When we don't see systems,

we fall out of the possibility of partnership with one another;

we misunderstand one another;

we make up stories about one another;

we have our myths and prejudices about one another;

we hurt and destroy one another;

we become antagonists when we could be collaborators;

we separate when we could remain together happily;

we become strangers when we could be friends;

we oppress one another when we could live in peace.

All of this happens without awareness or choice.

Four Types of System Blindness: Spatial, Temporal, Relational, and Process

We suffer from Spatial Blindness.

We see our part of the system

but not the whole;

we see what is happening with us

but not what is happening elsewhere;

we don't see what others' worlds are like,

the issues they are dealing with,

the stresses they are experiencing;

we don't see how our world impacts theirs

and how theirs impact ours;

we don't see how all the parts influence one another.

We suffer from Temporal Blindness.

We see the present

but not the past;

we know what we are experiencing *now*

but not what has led to these experiences;
we know our satisfactions and frustrations,
our feelings of closeness and distance,
the issues and choices and challenges we are currently facing.
All of this we experience in the present
but we don't see the history of the present,
the story of our system that has brought us to this point
in time.

We suffer from Relational Blindness.
In systems we exist only in relationship to one another:
we are sometimes Top to others' Bottom
and sometimes Bottom to others' Top;
we are sometimes Middle
torn between two or more Ends
and sometimes one of several Ends
tearing at a common Middle;
we are sometimes Provider to Customer
and sometimes Customer to Provider;
we are sometimes the Dominant over the Dominated
and sometimes the Dominated under the Dominant.
We don't see ourselves in relationship,
nor do we see the dances we fall into in relationship:
Becoming Burdened Tops
and Oppressed Bottoms,
Unsupported Ends
and Torn Middles,
Judged Providers
and Done-to Customers,
the Righteously Dominant
and the Righteously Dominated.

We suffer from Process Blindness.
We don't see our systems as wholes,
as entities in their environment.
We don't see the processes of the whole
as the whole struggles to survive.
We don't see how "It" differentiates
in an environment of shared responsibility and complexity
and how we fall into Turf Warfare with one another.
We don't see how "It" individuates
in a diffusing environment
and how we become Alienated from one another.
We don't see how "It" coalesces
in an environment of shared vulnerability
and how we become enmeshed in GroupThink with
one another.

Seeing Systems

This book is about seeing systems.
It is about overcoming System Blindness.
It is about seeing our part in the context of the whole (Act I).
It is about seeing the present in the context of the past (Act I).
It is about seeing ourselves in relationship with others and
creating satisfying and productive partnerships in these
relationships (Act II).
It is about seeing our systems' processes in ways that
enable us to create systems with extraordinary capacities
for surviving and developing (Act III).

The Power Lab and the Organization Workshop: My Windows to Systems

THE POWER LAB

The Elite (Tops)

Managers (Middles)

Immigrants (Bottoms)

Living Together in the Community of New Hope

My understanding of systems is a fortuitous outcome of work that had another goal. Over twenty-five years ago, I set out to create a learning environment in which people could deepen their understanding of power and powerlessness in social systems. The result was the Power & Systems Laboratory (now called the Power & Leadership Conference).

The basic idea was to create a societal setting in which people could *experience* issues of power and powerlessness directly and dramatically. And so we created a world with clearcut differences in power and resource control—a world somewhat ironically called the Community of New Hope.

There are three social classes in New Hope—the Elite (or Tops), who control the society's wealth and institutions, the Managers (or Middles), who manage the society's institutions for the Elite, and the Immigrants (or Bottoms), who enter the society with no funds, few resources, and no control over the society's institutions. This new world is compelling in that it encompasses all aspects of participants' lives—the quality of their housing and meals, the job opportunities available to them, the amount of money they have, their access to resources, and more.

A good play needs an appropriate theater, and we were fortunate early on to discover the Craigville Conference Center on Cape Cod. Craigville offered an isolated setting with a variety of housing possibilities for the various social classes and a huge tabernacle that could house the society's institutions—its court, newspaper, company store, employment center, pub, and theater. And most important, the Craigville staff have over the years functioned as patient, understanding, cooperative, sometimes bemused, partners in this venture.

We staff create the "world" into which participants are "born"—as either Elite, Managers, or Immigrants—and then we step back and allow the community to unfold. There are no scenarios to follow, no further directions from staff. What becomes of the society depends on whatever the collection of players makes of it.

The Power Lab was created to support participants in their learning about systems and power, but I have undoubtedly been its major beneficiary. Over the past twenty-five years, I have played a variety of roles in these Communities of New Hope, sometimes as an active player—Elite, Manager, or Immigrant—but most often, as an Anthropologist standing outside the system, collecting its history as it unfolds, observing, and interviewing societal members. It was not until several years had passed that I realized what a remarkable situation I had fallen into. How often does one have the opportunity to stand outside a social system and observe its total life—to be privy to the separate deliberations of each class as well as to their interactions with one another?

Several of the Scenes to follow come directly from the Power Labs (11. Bart and Barb, 12. 'Anthropology', 23. Daniel, 43. Alienation Among the Middles, 48. Immigrant Martha Has a Breakdown), but these Scenes are but the tip of the iceberg—*everything* in this book is infused with learning drawn from the Power Labs.

THE ORGANIZATION WORKSHOP

Tops (Executives)

Middles (Managers)

Bottoms (Workers)

Customers

Working Together in Creative Consultants, Inc. (CCI)

The Organization Workshop is an offshoot of the Power Lab. People who participated in the Power Labs began to request that we bring our work into their organizations. Apart from a few truly adventurous souls (Jim Stadelmaier, then at AT&T, for one), there was reluctance to do a full scale Power Lab in-house. However, there was considerable interest in helping Executives, Managers, and Workers deepen their understanding of systems and their ability to work cooperatively with one another. This interest set the stage for the development of the Organization Workshop.

Here again the educational strategy is to create a learning environment in which participants can directly experience key processes and dilemmas of organizational life. In this workshop, participants are "born" into an organization that exists for between a few hours and a day. The organization—Creative Consultants, Inc. (CCI)—is composed of Executives (Tops), who have overall responsibility for the system, a group of Managers (Middles), and several Worker groups (Bottoms), whose members work on various projects assigned by Tops or Middles. Outside the organization are potential Customers who have projects they need help on and money to pay for service. Here again staff simply set the stage; we put people into position, present the traditions of the organization, then step back and turn the organization loose.

In each workshop, there are several Times Out of Time (TOOTs) (see Scenes 8 and 9), in which we stop the organization, bring everyone together, and have them describe their experiences as Tops, Middles, Bottoms, and Customers: What are their worlds like? What pressures are they experiencing? How does each part of the system experience the other parts? These TOOTs tend to be incredibly illuminating experiences for participants. But consider for a moment what a remarkable learning opportunity the TOOTs have been for me—listening to many hundreds of people over the years as they describe their experiences as Tops, Middles, Bottoms, and Customers. For me, what light this has shed on the nature of systems! And my intention in this book is to share that light with you.

Swimmers, Slugs, and Ballet Notes: A Word About Style

As you may have already noticed, this book is written in a nontraditional form. There are Acts and Scenes, pinballs and talking body parts and mysterious "swimmers"; there are poems and dialogues along with conceptual material and cases; there are amebocytes and slugs and earthworms, a variety of dances, and even one set of ballet notes. The imagery of dance is used regularly because so many system processes seem balletic in nature: One party pulls up responsibility to himself or herself while the other passes it up; Bottom groups neatly and regularly split into the "reasonables" versus the "hardliners"; Middles fly apart from one another while Bottoms coalesce. There is form and coherence and predictability to all of these movements. None of which is to imply a lightness to these dances, because the dances I describe alienate us from one another, knock us out of the possibility of partnership, and sometimes lead to wholesale death and destruction (see Scene 31. The Terrible Dance of Power).

It is my fondest wish that you are enriched by the diversity provided in this book and that the various pieces come together to help you see more clearly the many systems of which you are a part. My wish is that in seeing systems in more depth, system life will become richer and more meaningful for you; that you will have a deeper understanding of your experiences in systems; that you will see new strategies for making happen what you want to have happen and what your systems need to have happen; that you will discover ways to create systems that contribute to the world and are deeply satisfying to you and other system members.

Acknowledgments

I offer my thanks to some very special people who, over the years through their encouragement, confrontation, support, and challenge, have contributed to this volume. Steven Piersanti—seeing the possibilities in an early, thin manuscript—gently yet unrelentingly urged me toward deeper levels of exploration. I am grateful to the Brookline Group—Lee Bolman, Dave Brown, Tim Hall, Bill Kahn, and Phil Mirvis—some of whom (I for one) have been meeting monthly for over fifteeen years to nourish, comfort, and prod one another toward greater self-awareness and personal and professional growth. The Power & Systems E-Team and Power Lab staff—Marcia Hyatt, Anne Litwin, Joe Meier, Mary Lou Michael, Jonathan Milton, Doug Pearson, Kevin Purcell, Bob Rehm, Michael Sales, and Joan Wofford—have been a great sustaining force throughout the process of writing this book. Warner Burke and Vlad Dupre offered unwavering support for my work during their tenures at the National Training Laboratories. Frank Basler, Lee Bolman (again), Bill Dickinson, and Andrea Markowitz contributed critical readings of early drafts of this book. I thank Edwin Mayhew for a delightful collaborative relationship as we developed workshop designs that led to the Organization Workshop, and Fritz Steele for our partnership during the early days of the Power Lab. The entire staff of the Craigville Conference Center—housekeeping, kitchen, grounds, directors, and front office—has worked diligently with us since 1972 to create the environment in which Power Labs have flourished. A very special thanks to Karen Ellis Oshry, my partner in all aspects of life, who has labored mightily by my side, tolerating my moods and reading and critiquing more variations of this work than any human being should ever be made to endure. I also want to thank Marty Kedian, Sir Speedy's man at the front line, who kept me at the top of his priorities, cranking out draft after draft of this work and always with a smile. Thanks to Erik Taros of EAT Design for cleaning up my hand drawn figures and making them computer friendly. And finally, I am indebted to the many thousands of people who have participated in our Power Labs and Organization Workshops and who have allowed me to be with them, observe them, and interview them as they wrestled with the challenges of system life. They came to me as students, but so much of the contents of this book I have learned from them.

As the Talmud says: From all my teachers I have learned. I thank you all for your contributions yet hold none of you responsible for the contents of this work.

Barry Oshry
Boston, Massachusetts
August 1995

SEEING THE BIG PICTURE

Act 1

Seeing the Part Without the Whole

Generally, if we are paying attention, we know what life is like for us in our part of the system. Other parts of the system are, for the most part, invisible to us. We do not know what others are experiencing, what their worlds are like, what issues they are dealing with, what dilemmas they are facing, what stresses they are undergoing. And what makes matters worse, sometimes we *think* we do know when, in fact, we do not. We have our beliefs, myths, and prejudices, which we accept as the truth and which become the bases of our actions. This blindness to other parts of the system—which we call *spatial blindness*—is a source of considerable misunderstanding and conflict.

Seeing the Present Without Seeing the Past

Temporal blindness refers to the fact that all current events in system life have a history; there is a coherent tale that has led to this particular point in time. Generally that history is invisible to us. We experience the present but are blind to the complex set of events that have brought us to the present. And again, it is this blindness to the history of the moment that is a source of considerable misunderstanding and conflict.

In Act One we experience the consequences of spatial and temporal blindness, and we explore strategies for seeing the big picture.

When we don't see the big picture . . .

1 Pinball

Sometimes life in the organization feels like a game of pinball,
and we're the little metal ball.
We start each day launched into a mysterious world of
bumpers
lights
bells
and whistles.
Lights flash on
and off.
Buzzers sound.
Gates open
and close,
sometimes propelling us at high speed to some other center
of the action,
and sometimes letting us drop quietly
into a hole.

All of this is a mystery to us.
Is this just a set of random events?
Or is there some grand scheme
known to others, but not to us?

One day we hit a bumper.
Lights flash.
Bells ring.
Big numbers go up on the scoreboard.
The next day we keep an eye out for that bumper.
We hit it.
Nothing. A dull thud.
And we continue, puzzled, along our way.

Some days there's lots of action
and big scores.
Other days there's lots of action
but not much of a score to show for it.
And other days there's very little of either.
At the end of the day—
lots of action
or little,
high scores
or low—
we drop through the final gate, heading home.
Sometimes we're impressed with our accomplishments,
sometimes depressed by our failures,
sometimes we're dreading the next launch,
sometimes we're champing at the bit for the next game.
And most times,
as we slide past the gate heading home,
we pause momentarily to reflect:
NOW WHAT WAS THAT ALL ABOUT?

2 The Manager of the Heart

Life in the organization may *feel* like a game of pinball,
but it works more like the human body.

And we're one small part—
maybe a fingernail
or a small corner of the brain—

or maybe we're an important part,
like the Manager of the Heart.

It's a peaceful job.
A nice even supply of fresh blood comes in from the lungs.
All engines pump smoothly: Lub . . . dub . . . lub . . . dub.

Oh oh! EMERGENCY! EMERGENCY!
Bells ring.
Buzzers sound.
Messengers come bursting into your office:
Chemical messengers from the bloodstream,
electrical messengers from nerve endings.
Who are these guys? Where do they get their information?
Who gives them the authority to tell you what to do?
"What emergency?" you ask. "Where?"
"There's no time to explain," say the Big Shot Messengers.
"JUST START SOME HEAVY PUMPING!"
So you tell your people: "FULL AHEAD ON THE PUMPS!"

You've got a good crew;
in no time they've got those pumps working away at full
capacity:
LUB . . . DUB . . . LUB . . . DUB.
You're proud of your crew. You turn to those Messengers and say:
"OK. Bring on that emergency. We can handle anything!"
But the Messengers aren't looking at you;
they're listening to their walkie-talkies.
"Forget it," says the electrical messenger.
"Cut back," says the chemical messenger.
"Emergency's canceled," they say.
"Emergency's canceled? We're just getting up a head of steam."
"CUT BACK! CUT BACK!" They're desperate now.

"YOU'LL BUST SOME PIPES!"
What'll I tell my crew?
"CUT BACK!!!!"

So you tell your crew.
"It's for the good of the system," you tell them.
"What do you want from me?" you ask them.
"I don't make the rules around here."

And then it's calm again.
A nice even flow of blood.
Pumps humming along: Lub . . . dub . . . lub . . . dub.
And you start thinking.

You start worrying about your crew.
How many changes of direction can these guys take?
Will I be able to count on them in a *real* emergency?

You start thinking about those Messengers,
those Specialists,
acting like big shots,
giving out orders,
all that technical mumbo jumbo.
When was the last time any of them bloodied their hands
opening and closing a stuck valve?

You start thinking about the Bigwigs.
Whoever they are,
wherever they are,
are they just playing games with us or what?
Maybe they know what they're doing,
maybe they don't.
What *do* they do up there all day anyhow?

Maybe *they've* got the big picture,
but what if they don't?
What if they're just . . . crazy?

And then you start thinking about yourself:
All this stress,
the way you blew up at those Messengers.
They're just doing their jobs after all.
Maybe you're losing your cool.
Maybe you can't cut it anymore.
Maybe you're not half the heart you used to be.

Oh oh! What's that sound?
Who's that racing along the bloodstream?
I know, I know.

EMERGENCY! EMERGENCY!

3 The Mystery of the Swim

In John Barth's *Night-Sea Journey*[1], a "swimmer" tells us of his journey.
He is the sole survivor of what began as a horde of eager, strong, and
dedicated swimmers—thousands of them, millions, maybe billions!
(He's not sure how many there were.) Only he remains—exhausted and
confused. The others are gone, drowned in what now seems like an
endless and pointless misadventure. Some, disillusioned and hopeless,
have taken their own lives.

Along the way, there were many debates among the swimmers.
What was this journey about? When did it begin? Where would it end?
What purpose, if any, did it serve?

Different camps with competing philosophies had developed regarding the meaning of the night-sea journey. Some argued that there was no meaning to it, that it was a pointless venture, that the struggles and deaths of the swimmers were all in vain. Many from this school took their own lives out of despair.

Others believed that the meaning of the venture lay in the swim itself, that the point of the swim was to swim as best one could for as long as one could.

Still others believed that the swim was part of some grand design that they, the swimmers, could only speculate about but never fully comprehend.

Within the grand design school, there were varying viewpoints: Some believed that the grand design was inherently good, others believed it was evil, and others believed it was neither good nor evil but that it merely existed.

But now all the others are gone; the debates, the discussions, the schools of philosophy have all drowned in the night sea. Only the narrator remains. We listen to him tell of his journey; he shares his thoughts and feelings. He is tired and confused. Should he continue the struggle or, like the others, allow himself to drown?

And as we readers listen, we too are confused and discomfited. The swimmer's story is an unsatisfactory one for us. The questions that plague him plague us too. What *is* this night-sea journey? Where did it begin? Where will it end? What purpose, if any, does it serve? The swimmer tells us in great detail about *his* journey; yet that is not enough for us. We need to comprehend the journey itself, the whole of which he is but a component part.

Barth never gives us the answer we seek, and without that answer, the journey remains for us an unsettling mystery.

However, if during our reading—the first, second, or third time through—it comes to us what this night-sea journey is, we are struck with great illumination. Now, having grasped the whole, we read the story through again. What once was confusing is now crystal clear; what once seemed complex and mysterious is now simple and straightforward. The squabbles, debates, and philosophical discussions all make sense to us. *And they all seem like so much silly superstition.*[2]

It strikes us: "Oh, what a difference it makes to see the swim we are in!"

And it is frightening to realize that we don't.

4 Seeing the Local Picture

Some systems are perfectly healthy
when viewed from the perspective of the whole;
but when viewed from the perspective of any one part,
they appear to be disorganized, chaotic, a collection of
random events.
Our Heart Manager didn't have the big picture.
All she knew about was what was happening in her small
piece of the system.
All she knew directly was that decisions affecting her were
being made in some remote power center.
She didn't know how those decisions were being made
and she didn't know whether to trust them.
She felt beleaguered by interference from a variety of staff
specialists.
She was concerned with potential labor unrest among her
troops,
who also did not have the big picture.
She was beset by rumors.
There was talk of a shutdown in the stomach during the
emergency.
Was it true? What did it mean? Would the heart be next?
For our Heart Manager, system life was a game of pinball.
When we have a local perspective:

- Things seem a lot messier than they really are or
  they seem a lot neater than they really are.
- We tend to blame ourselves for things that may not be our fault or
  we blame others for things that may not be their fault.
- We react to rumors rather than facts.
- We tend to misinterpret events happening elsewhere in the system.

- We tend to misunderstand and misjudge others in the system:

  We may see them as malicious, incompetent, and insensitive when, in fact, they are not.

  We may see them as well-meaning and all-wise when, in fact, they are not.

- We are unsure about ourselves, about what to do, about how our actions fit in with the actions of others and with the whole.

When we have a local perspective, organizational life feels like
a game of pinball . . . or worse.

5 "Stuff" Happens

We may be blind to others' worlds,
but this does not stop them from sending "stuff" our way.

Here you are going about your business

and then . . .
stuff happens.

Some of the stuff that comes our way is good news:
- We get the bonus we've been waiting for.
- The project is accepted.

Some of the stuff that comes our way is noxious:
- We don't like it.

Some of the stuff that comes our way is a mystery:

■ "Why on earth are they doing that?"

And some of the stuff that comes our way is
noxious *and* a mystery.

For example: You make what seems like a simple request of your
supervisor, and instead of saying, "Sure thing, you can count on it, it's
coming your way," your supervisor looks at his feet, shuffles around,
and mumbles, "Uh . . . well . . . let's see . . . er . . . well, I'll see what I
can do." Stuff.

You go to your workers with a proposal you think they will be
enthusiastic about, and instead, they put up a wall of resistance. Stuff.

You know that your customer is upset so you make a gesture to soothe the customer's feelings, and instead of appreciation, the customer replies with anger and sarcasm. Stuff.

You send a memo to your Top Executive making what you feel are valuable suggestions for improving the operation. Weeks go by, and there is no response to your memo. Stuff. (Physicists would probably refer to this as "minus stuff.")

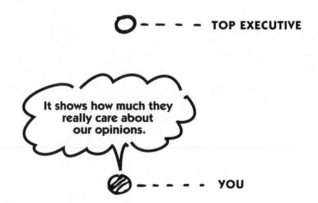

They send us stuff, and how do we react?

1. *We make up stories about it.* We don't like mysteries, so in the absence of knowledge about other people's worlds, we quickly fill the void with our stories about them. We create our myths about their motives, their competencies. And we don't see ourselves making up stories, we see our stories as the truth.

2. *We take it personally.* We experience the stuff as if it is aimed at us and intended to hurt or block us.

3. *We react to it.* We get mad, we get even, we withdraw.
   Our actions then become the stuff for others. They make up their
   myths about us—about our motives and competencies. They take
   our actions personally and react to us—getting mad, getting even,
   withdrawing—and on and on it goes when we do not see the
   worlds of others.

4. *And that is the end of partnership.*

6 Seeing Context
Much That Feels Personal Is Not Personal at All

The questions are:

What would we see if we could look into the worlds of others?

What new possibilities would open up for us?

In organizations, much of the time

we think we are dealing *person-to-person*

when, in fact, we are dealing *context-to-context.*

And much that feels personal

is not personal at all.

Top Living in a World of Complexity and Responsibility

When interacting with *Tops,*
we are dealing with people living in a world of
considerable *complexity*
(they have many difficult, ambiguous, unpredictable
issues to deal with)
and *responsibility*
(they are held accountable for the successes and failures
of the system).

So now that I can see into Top's world, I may have a better sense of what happened to my memo to the Top Executive suggesting improvements in the operation—why I've gotten no response. It may be that Top experienced my well-intentioned suggestion as just one more complication in an already overcomplicated life. It's also possible that Top, feeling responsible for the overall operation, experienced my cavalierly offered suggestion as a criticism.

It may also be that now that I see Top's world more clearly, I can come up with smarter strategies for getting my suggestions heard. How can I come across in a way that is seen as reducing the complexity of Top's world rather than increasing it? How can I come across in a way that communicates that I share responsibility for the system?

Bottom Living in a World of Invisibility and Vulnerability

When interacting with *Bottoms,*
we are dealing with people living in a world of
invisibility

(they often are not seen by higher-ups)
and *vulnerability*
(higher-ups can influence their lives in major and minor
ways).

Now that I see into Bottom's world, I may have a better idea of why my proposal was greeted by my workers with a wall of resistance. Higher-ups are always doing things to Bottoms: Reorganizing, lauching new initiatives, changing the health care plan, shutting down plants, relocating plants, merging with other companies. It's easy to see how my proposal was experienced as just another case of "Them doing it to us again." Now that I see into Bottom's world more clearly, it may be that I can come up with better strategies for gaining involvement. How can I acknowledge their experience of vulnerability? And how can my proposal reduce rather than increase that vulnerability?

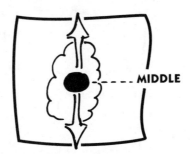

Middle Living in a Tearing World

When interacting with *Middles,*
we are dealing with people living in a *tearing* world
(they are pulled between you and others).
What you want from them, they don't have;
they need to go to others to get it.
And what others want from them,
they need to come to you to get.
They experience "simple" requests *from* you or others
as complex tearing *between* you and others.

Now that I see into Middle's world, I have a better understanding of why my Supervisor's response to me was so weak and wishy-washy. Because Middle doesn't have what I asked for, and because Middle would have to go to someone else to get it, it's crystal clear to me that my "simple" request is not so simple. It's easy to see how my request creates more tearing on Middle.

And it may be that now that I see into Middle's world, I can come up with more effective strategies for working with Middle to get what I need. How can I acknowledge the tearing on Middle, rather than poking fun at it or making it worse? How can I support Middle in getting what I need? How can I reduce the tearing rather than increase it?

Customer Living in a World of Neglect

When interacting with *Customers,*

we are dealing with people living in a world of *neglect*

(they receive inadequate attention;

products and services do

not come as fast as they want,

at the level of quality they want,

and at a satisfactory price).

Now that I see into Customer's world, I have a better understanding of why my Customer reacted to my nice gesture with anger and sarcasm. Customer was not interested in a tour of the facility. Customer was not interested in coffee and donuts. Customer was not interested in completing a customer satisfaction questionnaire. Customer was only interested in quality service, and quality service was not forthcoming.

It's easy to see how Customer experienced all of my nice gestures as more neglect.

And now that I can see my Customer's situation, I may be better able to develop the relationship both Customer and I want. How do I decrease Customer's experience of neglect rather than increase it?

■

Stuff happens.

We have two choices:

We can take the actions of others personally

and see what that gets us:

- Lots of good stories with good parts for US and bad parts for THEM
- Lots of evaluations
- Excuses
- Plenty of righteous indignation

Or

we can take their worlds into account.

What are *they* dealing with?

It may be harder work this second way:
- Less reflex
- More thought
- Less blame
- More compassion
- Less righteous indignation
- More power

It's our choice.

What possibilities open up for us when we are able to see into others' worlds?

1. We may have more understanding of others, more empathy with them.

2. We may be less quick to judge others, to see them as malicious, incompetent, insensitive.

3. We are in a better position to be strategic—to make happen what we want to have happen by taking other people's worlds into account.

7 The "Truth" About Jack

Jack is fired.

Jack's manager says:

"Jack was a pain in the butt, always complaining. The reorganization worked out perfectly. We no longer had any need for him. When I learned he was causing trouble for his group, that was the perfect opportunity to let him go. I asked the Tops if I could fire him, and they said go ahead."

One of Jack's co-workers says:

"I liked Jack. We were a tight group. I never saw him do anything wrong, nothing that would warrant firing. When I learned he was fired, I was scared: If they could fire him for whatever he did, then I wasn't safe either."

Jack's manager says:

"I was under pressure from the Tops. They were looking to me for production. There were Customers to satisfy, contracts to be signed, work to be done. The other group members were ready to work, but not Jack. Whenever I came to the group with work to be done, Jack always had these issues he *needed* to talk about. I just couldn't get the work done with him around."

A Customer says:

"When I learned that Jack was fired, I hired him immediately. I needed some creative help on my project and wasn't getting it. I never experienced Jack as a troublemaker. While working for me, he was a dedicated, hard-working, creative employee. As for the firing, all Jack ever wanted was respect. What was wrong with that?"

Jack says:

"In the beginning, the Manager asked us to come up with some creative ideas on a project. We put a lot of energy into that, and then we learned that the decision's been made and the Customer hadn't even *heard* our ideas. Then the Manager tells us we've been put on a *new* project. We start on that project, only to learn there's a reorganization and our group is being broken up. It's crazy, and I'm frustrated. I want us all to talk about what's been happening to us. But the Manager says there's no time for that; there's work to be done and the reorganization to be implemented. Finally, I'm given a new job: I'm going to do the design work for all the groups. I like that; it seems like a good assignment; I'm ready to go. Then I look around and see that *all the groups are doing their own design work!* I'm bewildered and totally frustrated. The next thing I know, I'm fired."

A second member of Jack's group says (sheepishly):

"I made a mistake. I was in the Men's room and I made a casual comment to the Manager about Jack being a problem. It was a joke, nothing serious. Jack wasn't any big problem for us, but you could see that he was aggravating the Manager. I made a joke about it—something to say in the Men's room. I never dreamt it would lead to this."

Jack's Manager says:
"That was all I needed."

A Top says to Jack's Manager:
"You think firing Jack was *your* idea? The Tops had already made

the decision to fire him. Here we were running around like crazy trying to keep this organization afloat. Every time I pass this guy in the hall—I mean *every* time—he's got some complaint: His equipment, the temperature, his work assignment, the Manager. Every time I pass him, it's another complaint. When you came into the office, we had already made the decision to fire him."

■

So what is the truth about Jack?

Is he a troublemaker? Or is he a regular group member not much different from the rest? Is he a whining complainer the organization best be rid of? Or is he an innocent, frustrated victim of management ineptitude? And what about that dedicated, hard-working, creative employee the Customer saw? Is that the real Jack?

The truth about Jack? Well, it depends as much on the conditions of *your* world as it does on who *he* is.

- In the world of a harried Top overwhelmed by complexity and responsibility, the truth is that Jack is an unnecessary complication.
- In the world of a Middle torn between pressures from above and below, the truth is that Jack's "simple request for conversation" is more unwelcome tearing.
- In the world of Jack's associate group members who share his condition of invisibility and vulnerability, the truth is that Jack is an OK guy not much different from the rest.
- In the world of a Customer starved for service, the truth is that Jack is the answer to your prayers.

Jack was fired. To what effect? Again it depends on where you stand.

The firing simplified the life of Tops,
it reduced the tearing of Middles,
it heightened the vulnerability of Bottoms,
and it resulted in much needed service for the Customer.

But doesn't this tell us more about *the others' worlds* than it does about Jack?

An old proverb says: "We see people not as *they* are but as *we* are." To which we add: "And who we are is shaped by the context in which we exist." We win first prize when we are able to see not just the actions of others, but also the context out of which these actions come. We win second prize (and it is not an inconsequential prize) when we know that, for the most part, we don't.

8 Times Out of Time

How can we see the big picture in our day-to-day system life—within the context of our family, our work group, our organization? It may be that life needs to imitate art. Let me share with you a dilemma I experienced in the early days of the Organization Workshop (see page XVII). We would set up the organization—with Tops, Middles, Bottoms, and Customers—and turn it loose. Action would break out all over the place—interactions within groups and across groups. I would run anxiously from place to place with my yellow pad, trying to track the action. After all, I was the one who set up this exercise, so it was important that I understand what was happening in order to help others learn from it. It was impossible. I couldn't keep up with the action; too much was happening in too many different locations. And even if I could see it all—which I couldn't—there was important information that was invisible to me. I had no access to people's experiences—what were they thinking and feeling? How were they experiencing their worlds? How were they experiencing people in other parts of the system? Eventually we solved the problem by creating the Time Out of Time (TOOT). And having created it, it became clear that it was less important that *I* saw what was happening throughout the system than that all system members saw it. So let's see how the TOOT works.

"Stuff" happens!

The exercise begins . . . and "stuff" happens. Everywhere. Tops aren't getting the information they need; Middles and Bottoms aren't getting the direction they need; Customers aren't getting the attention they need; work on projects gets started, is taken away, and disappears into a black hole; the organization appears to be disjointed; Middles can't get their act together, there are imbalances, some projects are drawing lots of attention, others are getting little or none; Tops are invisible to Bottoms, who wonder what, if anything, Tops do; reorganizations happen, and many wonder: Why?; Bottoms are wondering what, if anything, is the added value of Middles?; Tops are deluged by demands coming from every direction; Bottoms get bonuses that they feel they don't deserve or they don't get bonuses that they feel they *do* deserve. It's another day in the whitewater. Emotions run the full gamut—from excitement and challenge to anger, despair, hopelessness, apathy. And then it's time to TOOT.

We stop the organization, bring all the players into one place, and ask them to describe for one another what life is like in their part of the system: *Describe your world for us. What are the issues you are dealing with? What are you feeling? How are you seeing other parts of the system? Are they helping you or hindering you?*

First we hear from the Tops, then the Bottoms, then the Middles, and finally the Customers. Each part of the system begins to elucidate its world for the benefit of the others. Together they begin to illuminate the whole.

The TOOTs are an impactful part of the workshop. They are clearly the antidotes to spatial blindness. It is as if someone has turned on the lights for the entire system. Myths about others begin to melt away. The worker who was so evaluative of the Middle gains a better appreciation of the dilemmas Middle lives with; Tops hear firsthand about the frustrations of Workers; everyone hears the frustrations of Customers; the processes within groups are illuminated—the turf issues developing among the Tops, the inability of Middles to get together, the *We* versus *Them* mentality developing among the Bottoms.

We set two basic guidelines for the TOOTs. *Tell the truth* (paint a picture for us; you are our experts on your part of the system; there is no other way for us to know what your world is like) and *listen carefully to others* (don't argue or debate, just let it in).

The TOOT's success depends on these two conditions:

- Are people willing and able to tell the truth of their experiences? (In highly political systems in which people are committed to keeping secrets from one another, TOOTs will not work. Likewise, the quality of TOOTs suffer when people are unable to get in touch with or share their experiences.)
- Are people willing and able to let in and accept as valid the experiences of others? (The value of the TOOT will be diminished if people are committed to maintaining their stereotypes of others even in the face of disconfirming evidence.)

When the two conditions are met, the results can be astounding. Some outcomes:

1. *Illumination.* It is intrinsically interesting for people to move beyond their narrow perspective to see "the big picture."

2. *Empathy.* People begin to have more empathy, understanding, and patience with one another. They are less quick to judge.

3. *Depersonalization.* As people begin to see the contexts of others' actions—the issues *they* are dealing with—they are less apt to take these actions personally. They realize: This is not an act directed against me.

4. *Revitalization.* Instead of reacting to others—getting mad at them, getting even with them, withdrawing—people put more of their energy into the work of the system.

5. *Problem solving.* Although it is *not* the purpose of the TOOT to solve problems, problems *are* identified—Tops are not getting the information they need; Customers are dissatisfied; efforts are being duplicated—and often, following the TOOT, these problems are addressed.

6. *Strategic planning.* As people begin to understand others' worlds, they see how their own actions have made it difficult for others to cooperate with them; and they see how they might get what they need by easing rather than exacerbating the conditions of others.

The TOOT Challenge

TOOTs are a possibility within most systems—the family, the work group, the plant, the business unit. Even when we work side by side with others, we are often blind to their experiences. We see the externals but not the internals; we see others' actions but not their thoughts and feelings.

The TOOT is a simple and powerful way to see the systems of which we are a part. All that is required is that we come together, share our experiences, and listen to the experiences of others.

What I appreciate most about the TOOT is that it is not prescriptive—you do not tell people what they should or should not do. The TOOT illuminates the system and, in that clarity, people see new choices. And the choices are theirs to make. Once we see clearly, most of us will do the right thing.

Our situation changes from one of blind reflex to enlightened choice.

TOOT GUIDELINES

1. EVERYONE SHOWS UP. It is important that all relevant parties be at the TOOT. Whether you are satisfied or dissatisfied, ready for new challenges or ready to quit, your experience is relevant to the TOOT. Come and be prepared to share your experience.

2. NO BUSINESS. The TOOT is not a staff meeting; it is not a time to solve problems (although what comes out at the TOOT often leads to subsequent problem solving). The purpose of the TOOT is to illuminate the system for all, so everyone can be clearer about the whole: What issues are people facing throughout the system?

3. TELL THE TRUTH. You are the expert on your part of the system. The rest of us are dependent on you to let us know what life is like for you in your part of the system: What your world is. What issues you are dealing with. What your feelings are.

4. LISTEN CAREFULLY TO OTHERS. Be open to the experiences of others. Discover what their worlds are like, their feelings, the issues they are facing.

9 The TOOT Dilemma

The TOOT is like turning a light on in a dark room when you thought the light was *already* on.

The TOOT confronts us with a dilemma:
We can listen to these others,
try to understand their worlds,
empathize with them,
work with them,
see them as OK people—
like us—
take their worlds into account,
try to ease their condition
just as we would like them to ease ours.

Or

we can stick with *our* story.

Our story may be more appealing than the TOOT story,

more dramatic,

bad guys (them),

good guys (us),

the blamed

and the blameless.

This is the tension the TOOT creates:

Our story

against ITs story,

judgment

against empathy,

blame

against understanding,

reaction

against thought,

"them"

against "all of us,"

good guys and bad guys

against just plain folks.

This is the tension of seeing systems.

You want to see your system?

Try TOOTs.

The challenge is this:

Are you willing to tell the truth?

Are you willing to listen to others?

Are you willing to give up your story

for ITs story?

Spatial blindness

is about

seeing the part

without the whole.

Temporal blindness

is about

seeing the present

without the past.

10 The Invisible Histories of the Swims We Are In

Several years ago, Karen Oshry, Joe Meier, and I set about what we thought would be a simple task. We were going to assemble a photo history of one of our Power Labs (the Elite, Managers, and Immigrants living together in the community of New Hope, see page XV)—twenty or so snapshots of events along with brief commentaries. *Three years later we completed the project!* (In fairness to us, not all of our time was spent on this project, but we spent considerably more time than we had anticipated.) Our plan at the outset was simple: Identify certain key events, match up the pictures, provide a few illuminating descriptions, and that would be that. Unfortunately, there are no isolated events in systems. Everything connects with everything else. We would identify a particular interaction and then get curious about what had led to it and what had followed from it. Each discovery led us to other questions and other discoveries. In the end, there was a story, a 300-page history, a clear and coherent picture of the life of this social system.[3]

From our outside perspective, this was a beautiful story—beautiful in that it had form, direction, movement, and clearly evolving patterns of interaction within and across the classes. This was not a set of random events, it was a story that was going someplace; yet in the living of that history, no system member had experienced its beauty. For them life was pretty much as we experience it daily—a collection of random events, or loosely connected events, ups and downs, rather than a richly textured unfolding story.

From this and many other experiences that followed, I am led to the hypothesis that, *in all systems there is a story that unfolds*—a history that has shape, movement, pattern, and direction. Each of our families has a coherent history—an unfolding tale about how each of us got to this point in time. Each of us is in touch with various pieces of our history, but the histories of our families as wholes tend to be invisible to us. And this is true for our work teams, our circles of friends, our task forces and organizations, and all the social systems of which we are a part. The histories of the "swims" we are in are invisible to us. Yet those histories are keys to our experiences in the swim.

The question regarding seeing systems is this: Can we see our system stories as they unfold? And if so, what difference can that "seeing" make?

What follows are pieces of two stories:

"Bart and Barb" communicates in encapsulated form what I mean by a beautiful story: No one sets out to create a story, yet a story emerges. The dramatic form of the story is as follows: Two members of the Elite struggle over the direction the society will take. First one member becomes dominant while the other is suppressed; then the second becomes dominant while the first is suppressed. Then the society splits and two distinctly different societies emerge, one for each Elite. The original society disappears; members dissatisfied with one society find a more suitable place for themselves in the other. In the end there is a total transformation of the original society. This is a history with a direction, an unfolding. Neither Bart nor Barb nor any of the other members of this system experience its beauty, form, shape, or coherence. They all have their good and bad moments, their joys and frustrations, their attractions to one another, and their hostilities. But the story of the whole is invisible.

"Bart and Barb" makes us wonder about our own systems: What are their stories? And if we could see those stories, how would that deepen our experience of our systems?

In "'Anthropology' or Mick Gets Wiped Out" we see the cost of temporal blindness: A Middle breaks down and drops out of society. The causes of this breakdown are invisible to all until the history is revealed, and then they are crystal clear. Anthropology reveals some of the history of this incident; it also gives us a glimpse into the processes used in the Power Lab to weave together a system's history. This piece raises a dilemma for us. We see the powerful impact our systems' histories can have; we see the potential that lies in revealing our histories; and we see what an immense challenge we face in doing so.

Anthropology, as described here, is probably not the most effective technology for helping members fully experience the rich flow and interconnectedness of their system lives. Our work suggests that members need to be more directly involved in unraveling their own history (see "Immigrant Martha Has a Breakdown" on page XX). The Anthropologist's central function may be to help in identifying key events and interactions along the way and in providing processes whereby system members can keep ongoing records of their experiences. "Applied Anthropology: Unraveling System History," the last item in this section, offers some guidelines for the process.

The Traditionalist and the Humanist

Bart and Barb are the central players in the Elite,
co-captains of the ship,
battling with one another over the course the ship
should take.

Louis and Minnie—
other members of the Elite—
are ballast in the hold,
shifting from side to side,
sometimes toward Bart,
sometimes toward Barb.

Bart is Traditionalist,
striving to maintain the system as he found it:
a harsh system,
a system of Haves and Have Nots.
All power rests with the Elite—
the Robe of Justice,
the Food,
the Housing,
Work, Information, Culture—
all controlled by the Elite.

Barb is Humanitarian,
a seer of new possibilities.
"We are the Elite," she says.
"We are not stuck with the past;
we can create a new world.
No need to be harsh.

We can take care of people,
make decisions *with* them,
share our power *with* them."

Bart fears Barb.
"We'll have to watch you closely," he says.
"You're dangerous.
You'll turn our world upside down.
Chaos."

Barb feels controlled by Bart.
"Lighten up," she says.
"Give," she says.
"Why not give?
What harm will it do?"

"Chaos," says Bart.
"Chaos might not be so bad," says Barb.

The ballast slides toward Bart.
Louis and Minnie agree:
Barb is a danger,
she must be controlled.
A rule is created:
An Elite can be ejected from the Elite
by the vote of three other Elites.
(Watch out for rules that control others;
they may come back for you.)

The ship heads out along Bart's course—
Tradition—
the way it is is the way it was.
Barb is captive on her own ship,
a reluctant Elite,

confused,
depressed,
beaten,
purposeless.

Barb Fights Back

Barb fights back from depression and defeat;
she struggles to change the system from within;
she struggles against Bart;
she is the voice of reason,
flexibility,
change,
hope—
a message of some appeal
to some Have Nots.

The ballast shifts toward Barb.
Louis and Minnie
support Barb's liberalizing efforts
while undermining Bart
and his Robes
and his Court
and his calls for Tradition.
The ship shifts course,
heading out along Barb's direction.
Now Bart is captive on the ship;
his Robes are laughed at,
his pronouncements ignored.

He fights for Tradition;
he is scoffed at,
publicly disowned by the Elite.
His rule is used against him;
he is voted out of the Elite.

Bart is confused,
depressed,
beaten,
purposeless.

Bart Fights Back

Bart fights back from depression and defeat.
He separates from Barb and Louis and Minnie;
he takes a piece of Elite property for himself;
he establishes a new society.
So now there are two societies—
and they are such different societies.
Take your choice:
It's Barb
or Bart.

The Hill and the Slum

Barb's society is the Hill—
uptown,
the big house,
overlooking the ocean,
food, money,
seriousness,
a yearning for higher purpose.

Bart's society is the Slum—
downtown,
dark and messy,
smoky, very smoky,
wine and beer,
playfulness,
and aimlessness.

Barb's leadership is purposeful;
Bart's is formless,
wandering,
chaotic (one might say).

Barb's society seeks higher meaning—
some cause "out there"
that we can serve.

Bart's society is primal:
How do we get more beer and wine
and cigarettes?
An all-night dance hall?
Games to play?

Barb's society
moves out to find a cause.
Bart's society
moves out to hustle cigarettes
and cash in empties.

Barb's society attracts one disgruntled Immigrant,
who, with Barb, finds meaning.
Bart's society attracts one overworked Middle,
who, with Bart, finds freedom.

The Middles "dis-integrate" perfectly:
one joins Barb;
one joins Bart;
one joins neither.

The Society Blossoms

The society has blossomed
like a flower—
beautifully,
symmetrically,
miraculously.
Everyone has found a place.
What could be more perfect?

That's how it looks from the outside.
And from the inside?

Bart and Barb cross paths on the street:
Barb looking for supplies;
Bart looking for fun.
"Barb!" Bart cries happily.
Barb looks away.
"Wanna play pictionary?!" cries Bart excitedly.
"F— off!" shouts Barb
purposefully.

What difference would it make

if we could see the unfolding stories

of our various system lives—

the family,

the organization,

the community,

our circle of friends—

if we could see

how we and others

got to this point in time?

What difference would it make

if we could see the day-to-day events of life

not as isolated events

but as pieces of a rich tale

with form,

and pattern,

and direction?

12 "Anthropology" or Mick Gets Wiped Out

CENTRAL CHARACTERS

Elites: Eddy, Ernest, Evelyn

Middles: Mick, Moira

Immigrants: Betty, Bob

Anthropologists: Barry, Gisela, Jonathan

Part I Wipeout

Mick was a Middle in one of our Power Labs. After two days on the job, he quit. He quit the society and he quit the program. Mick left in a fury. He would neither talk nor listen to anyone. He simply walked off. A day later we heard from Mick. He was still in the area, emotionally unsteady ("I can't go home in this shape").

Let me assure the concerned reader that Mick returned to the program, and at program's end, he was completely healed, in high spirits, and delightfully enlightened regarding the travails of Middles in organizations. What troubles me is that the special conditions of the laboratory made this healing and enlightenment possible, and these same conditions do not exist for the hordes of Middles in organizations who are being "wiped out" daily.

Let's look at the events that led up to Mick's breakdown. As a Middle in the Power Lab, Mick functioned between the Elite who owned and controlled most of the society's resources and institutions and the Immigrants who entered the society with little more than the clothes on their backs.

Much of Mick's time was spent navigating between pressures from the impoverished Immigrants to change the system and those from the Elite to maintain it. Mick's job was complex; he was living in a downsized system that required him to wear several hats. He was responsible for the Employment Center: lining up full- and part-time jobs for the Immigrant laborers, scheduling work, and serving as Paymaster. He also was the Work Supervisor and the society's Police Chief. The work/police combination regularly put him at odds with himself. ("As Police Chief I'm inclined to enforce the law; however, doing so can have negative consequences for my Workers' morale.")

Mick had been a diligent Middle—never shirking his many and complex duties. And he was scrupulously even-handed. When dealing with the Immigrants, he upheld the Elite's rules and standards. ("No, I don't believe you are entitled to a bed or a meal without paying for it". And when dealing with the Elite, he consistently carried forth concern for the Immigrants' position. ("All they want is to be heard by you.")

Mick was crunched in the middle. He was angry at the Immigrants. ("Sometimes I feel the same way with my kids. If they dropped off the face of the earth, I wouldn't care. You give and you give and you give, and it becomes an entitlement. Even when the Immigrants say they want to help us, it's really that they want something from us.") And he felt consistently undermined by the Elite. ("We have people who break the rules, and you Elite don't do anything about it. As Police Chief I have things to enforce, but there's no backup from you. It's a joke. The Immigrants say 'If we hold out long enough, the Elite will give in.'")

Now to the triggering event: The Elite came to Mick with a proposition. They had a piece of property they were willing to make available to the Immigrants. This was a major move. The new house was to serve two purposes: To relieve overcrowding and to provide space for a new societal institution.

Mick was concerned that the house was going to be seen by the Immigrants as another victory. ("They bark we jump, they bark we jump.") He wanted the Elite's agreement that *he* would manage the process, that it would not be tossed in by the Elite over the Middles' heads. Mick said to the Elite: "What's even more important to the Immigrants than the house is that they have a say."

The conversation with the Elite went on for close to an hour. The Elite proposed that Bob (an Immigrant) co-manage the process with Mick. "No," said Mick. "Bob reports to me. It would undermine me. I need to manage the process." And so it was agreed. The house would be put into play; Mick was to manage the process; the Elite would not undermine him.

Twenty minutes later Mick was meeting with the Immigrants. He told them about this new piece of property that was becoming available.

He told them that the Elite were hoping this would have an uplifting effect on the community. He told them that it was up to them to decide how to use the house, how to manage the process. Mick believed he was coming in with a big piece of news until he was interrupted in mid-sentence by Immigrant Bob: "I want you to know," says Bob, "that the Elite have agreed to meet with Betty and me on that very same subject in fifteen minutes."

Mick gulped. He was clearly shaken. He gamely went on with the rest of his agenda, but he had just been wiped out. The next morning he quit the society and the lab.

Part II   A Simple Explanation

This appears to be a straightforward tale of betrayal. Mick has been a hardworking Middle, laboring to adjust to the incompatible demands of the Elite and the Immigrants. He has been under considerable pressure from both sides. He is angry at the Immigrants and he feels unsupported and undermined by the Elite. He finally manages to establish a solid set of agreements with the Elite, and within the hour, those agreements are broken. He is to bring the good news to the Immigrants, but they already have the news. He alone is to manage the process, but now it appears to be in the hands of two of his employees. Mick's emotions are complex—his rage at both the Immigrants and the Elite is beyond his usual coping range. At the same time, he blames himself. ("I was given a simple task. If only I did it right. I feel like a failure.") And finally he feels that the Mick he knew has disappeared in this process. ("Where did I lose myself? I lost me in this process.")

Part III   "Anthropology"

Things are not as they seem. There is quite a different story to be told here, a startling story. Everything that I described did happen just as I described it, yet this is one small piece of the truth. For example: What if I told you that there was no betrayal here? Would you believe me?

First, let me tell you how we know what we know. At the Power Lab, we have a team of "Anthropologists." The job of this team is to keep the history of the society as it unfolds. It is a grueling job— "Anthros" are usually the first to rise in the morning and the last to retire at night. They go around with heavy notebooks and a supply of pens. Their assignment is to be everywhere—to observe, to record conversations, to summarize events. One thing they are clearly told *not* to do is to interpret events or evaluate them. Simply witness. Observe. Interview. Write and write and write. Stay close to the facts. Don't jump too quickly to patterns. Don't even look for patterns. Stick to the data, and pray that the patterns will emerge.

Anthropology is possible at the Power Lab because of the contract Anthros make with participants: "We have access to everything. No meetings—no matter how private—are closed to Anthros." But, because the Power Lab is by design a very political system, we promise confidentiality: "Information from one part of the system will not be passed on to people in other parts of the system. This information will only be used once the societal experience has ended." It is only through such a compact that we gain the access we need to gather the system's history.

It very quickly becomes clear why such a contract would be difficult to establish in most other systems. The commitment to be a true "Learning Organization" would have to be quite strong.

Consider, for example, a conversation I witnessed among Human Resources executives: A strike was impending at one plant. The Human Resource executive said, with a sheepish grin, "To tell the truth, we could take a strike. That would give us the opportunity to shut the plant down and move to the Midwest, closer to headquarters and cheaper labor." So, while the union worked on strategies for squeezing management, management waited, only too eager to be squeezed. This was information that management in that organization was not about to make available to a roving Anthropologist, knowing that eventually it would be revealed.

This type of Anthropology can be a powerful tool for deepening our understanding of social system life. It has great potential for illuminating life for system members; and for most systems, it would require an immense shift in thinking about openness and secrecy.

And so the following story emerges only because three Anthropologists—Jonathan, Gisela, and myself—happened to be stationed at various locations, notebooks and pens in hand, as the tale unfolded.

Part IV   An Arm's Length Elite

As the society was unfolding, we Anthros were struggling to identify the Elite pattern. It was frustrating. There were so little data. We looked for meetings of the Elite, but there were few such meetings, and very little business transpired at whatever meetings there were. There were no momentous battles among the Elite (an infrequent pattern as Elites with differing opinions as to how the system should go typically battle with one another for control. See Scene 38.). So these Elites were not a closely knit team, nor were they enmeshed in turf battles. *Then it struck us how the absence of data was the data.* These were arm's length Elite. Each had his or her area of responsibility, which each oversaw with relatively little interaction with the others. There were striking differences among the Elite in their personal styles and visions for the society. These differences were briefly confronted at the beginning of their life together, but not thereafter.

Two of the Elites, Eddie and Ernest, had sharply contrasting styles. Eddie valued energy, his own and others. He operated intuitively. He did not need complex, well thought-out rationales for action. He was comfortable stirring things up. He had little need to please the Immigrants or to feel personally responsible for improving their conditions. Ernest was much more rational in his thinking—even if things *felt* right, that was not sufficient evidence to prove that they *were* right. Ernest needed rationales and frameworks within which his and others' actions fit. Ernest and Eddie had strong negative feelings toward one another, feelings that were played out in action but not confronted head-on.

Evelyn, the third member of the Elite, stayed clear of the tension between Eddie and Ernest. She quietly went about her business—organizing the complex relationships with the dining room—good at details, arranging, cleaning up.

Periodically an Anthropologist would capture a graphic image of this arm's length Elite pattern (not yet realizing that it *was* a pattern). We would trudge up to the Elite house, hoping to find some interaction to capture. (What are you going to write in your notebook if no one is talking?) Instead of interaction, there would be Ernest in his car, on the car phone, talking to his family. Inside the house, Evelyn was sitting in the living room, waiting for Eddie. Upstairs Eddie was reading in bed. When Evelyn finally moved upstairs and found Eddie, they carried on a brief conversation at a distance of approximately fifteen feet—Evelyn in the doorway, Eddie lying in bed.

In your Anthropologist's notebook, all of this makes for fairly dull reading. Only later does its significance become clear.

Part V The Anthropologists' Ordeal: Capturing the System's Story

Before unravelling the story of Mick's wipeout, we need to talk more about the unravelling process. We Anthropologists have a very specific assignment. Toward the end of each Power Lab we are given a two- to three-hour time slot with a specific agenda: To help participants see the totality of the system of which they have been a part. Our assignment is to capture the system's story in some coherent fashion that illuminates the experiences of the individuals within it. We are given twenty-four hours to complete our task. We closet ourselves. Among us we have over 500 pages of handwritten notes: snatches of conversation—no interpretations, no evaluations, only who said what to whom. Many of our notes are barely legible or are illegible. They are hastily written. Sometimes there are too many people talking at once, or we have recorded conversations among people walking from one place to another (try writing while walking). There may have been conversations held in the rain or in the dark. We have no notes on apparently key events that happened when none of us was present. There were more discrete events than we had Anthropologists to cover them. There were times when we were so fatigued that we just stopped writing. We are overwhelmed by the size of the our task and by our limitations.

At the outset, the process is fascinating. It is a remarkable experience—a rare privilege—to stand outside a system with these relics and fossils of existence and bring to life a coherent whole. In time reality strikes . . . then panic! We are proceeding too slowly. A quarter of our preparation time is gone, and we have covered merely an eighth of the system's life. We need to speed it up. We briefly entertain certain illusions—we can skip certain parts; we can focus only on *important* events. We try; we fail. We are trapped in our own systemic thinking. We jump ahead only to find that in order to understand "ahead" we need to back up. Everything connects with everything else. There are no shortcuts. So we plow on.

We do not get to the immediate events surrounding Mick's wipe-out until 2:00 A.M. Until then we think we have a clear picture of what happened. Ernest and Evelyn had betrayed Mick. They promised him that he could manage the new house deal; they promised that they would not undermine him; then they betrayed him. When we saw what really happened, there was a collective gasp from the Anthropologists.

Part VI   When Agendas Collide

It is 2:00 A.M. The Anthroplogists are reviewing their notes covering the evening events leading up to Mick's wipeout. The supposed big news of the early evening is the discrepancy in dinner menus. The Elite had chosen not to eat in the dining room (the usual arrangement); instead they had their dinner—lobster with fixings accompanied by wine—delivered to their home. Meanwhile the Immigrants, only able to afford the Class B dinner, made do with franks and beans. Once again, however, the story is revealed not in the grand gesture but in the sideline and apparently less significant events. When all of these were pieced together, the following story unfolded.

The Elite were having their lobster dinner at their house. Gisela's sense was that nothing of importance happened at dinner. The conversation was subdued. As usual there was little talk of business, and no decisions were made. The conversation took a lighthearted turn as the Elite began to play with fantasies of how they might use their as yet unused piece of property: As a monastery for one of the more trouble-some Immigrants; as a retreat house for women; as a center for the arts. [You, the reader, know the potential significance of this lighthearted conversation, because you know that the management of the new house became a central issue. But, at the time and without foreknowledge, the discussion seemed unimportant, lighthearted dinner joviality—particu-larly because the subject was eventually simply dropped. It is possible that the conversation might not even have made it into your notebook.]

Keep in mind: These are our arm's length Elite.

Jonathan had been with the Immigrants at their franks and beans dinner. Here the conversation centered around whether the Immigrants could remain a unified group and, at the same time, allow and encour-age individual members to pursue their own paths. Unbridled individu-ation became the theme. Some members were to work for change with-in the system; one was planning middle-of-the-night direct action against the Elite; and two (Bob and Betty) were setting out to explore entrepreneurial possibilities.

So now two stories began to unfold around our arm's length Elite.

Jonathan tagged along with Bob and Betty as they sought out Eddie. ("Are there any entrepreneurial opportunities in this community?") While Barry came across Ernest and Evelyn talking about the possibilities of an Art House. [As the reader, you are now enjoying the global view; you probably have some good hunches as to how this scenario will unfold. As on-the-ground Anthropologists, however, we saw no pattern. Each of us was out there doing our job, writing it all down, not knowing whether the piece we were describing was worth the ink we were using.]

Immigrants Betty and Bob approached Elite Eddie looking for entrepreneurial opportunities. Eddie dangled the possibility of the house in front of them. He talked about being willing to entertain serious proposals. "There *is* a window of opportunity," he said, "but it will close quickly."

Meanwhile Barry stood by as Elites Evelyn and Ernest (at the usual arm's length from Eddie) were also thinking about the unused house. They formulated their own plan for bringing it into play, and an explicit part of their strategy was to involve the Middle Managers, Mick and Moira. Evelyn said, "I want to give them the resources they've been looking for."

And now two independent streams of events, which began at arm's length, hurtled toward collision (a terrible mixing of metaphors).

Immigrants Bob and Betty went off to do some thinking about the new house, and they scheduled a follow-up meeting with Elite Eddie. At the same time, Elites Evelyn and Ernest brought their plan to Mick and Moira.

Mick worked out his agreements with Evelyn and Ernest (he'd manage the process; no undermining from the Elite). At the same time, Bob and Betty rejoined their group feeling some confidence that *they* could make a deal for the house.

Mick went to the Immigrants and made his "surprise" announcement, only to find out that Betty and Bob—his employees—were already working on their own deal.

Wipeout!

Part VII More Pieces of the Puzzle

It's 2:30 A.M. We Anthropologists think we have this fairly well figured out, but there is still a puzzle. Why did Ernest and Evelyn allow this to happen? How could they have so easily violated the agreement they had made with Mick? We go back into our notebooks.

Gisela was at a late-night meeting involving Bob and Betty and all of the Elites. Ernest and Evelyn were there; they were watching Eddie complete his deal with Immigrants Betty and Bob. Why didn't Ernest and Evelyn stop this? Why didn't they talk about the agreement they had made with Mick just hours before?

Barry noted that when Immigrants Betty and Bob left the Immigrant meeting to meet with Elite Eddie, Middle Moira went with them. And Mick, still reeling from the shock of his "betrayal," in a last gasp of Middle other-devotedness, said to Moira, "Whatever you do, I want you to support them (Betty and Bob)."

Gisela noted that when all of the Elite met with Bob and Betty, Moira also was there; and she announced, "I am representing Mick."

"I am representing Mick." Puzzle piece added to piece added to piece until . . . another communal gasp escaped from the collective Anthropologist throat. Aha! There was no betrayal.

So here is the scene. It was a late-night meeting. The purpose was to conclude negotiations for the new house. Present were all of the Elite: Eddie, Evelyn, and Ernest. Also present were two Immigrants: Bob and Betty. And there was Middle Moira. Middle Moira explained her presence at this meeting as representing Mick.

To Elite Eddie, this meeting was the culmination of his deal with Immigrants Betty and Bob.

To Elites Evelyn and Ernest, this was the culmination of *their* deal with Mick. To their way of thinking, *Moira was there representing Mick.* To their way of thinking, Mick must have made his presentation to the Immigrants, Bob and Betty had picked up on it, and this meeting was the natural outcome. Mick *was* managing the process, just as they had agreed he would.

So, according to everyone but Mick, there was no wipeout. When Mick left the program, it was just a case of personal instability. Case closed!

Part VIII   Without Anthropologists

If there had been no Anthropologists, what would the story have been?

Mick was wiped out.

He had a clear picture of how it happened. He was betrayed. His picture, however, was grossly inaccurate and incomplete. He was furious at the others; he was confused; and he focused much of the blame on himself. ("I was given a simple task and I failed.")

The Elites' absolutely central role in the wipeout was invisible to them. *Their arm's length pattern was undoubtedly the single most powerful determinant in this scenario,* yet they were unlikely to see it. They had other explanations: Too much stress, immaturity, or maybe the antisocial actions of certain Immigrants. (Remember the Immigrant who was planning some late-night harassment? Well he did it. And he harassed the Middles' house as well as the Elites'. Maybe that was what drove Mick over the edge?) There would probably be well-intentioned feedback to Mick (it's called Performance Management) about his managerial weaknesses and how to function more effectively. And Mick would likely take this feedback to heart. More attention to personal and professional development. That's the answer.

Part IX   What Can We Do with This Knowledge?

There is some powerful knowledge here, but what can we do with it? We are blind to system history, and as a consequence, we are at its mercy. This is one case of a wipeout that occurred because of system blindness. Because of our blindness, personal breakdowns happen; because of our blindness, we conjure up wrong explanations; because of our blindness, we propose misguided remedial actions.

In one respect, Mick's story is a rarity because we have been able to see the blindness. But do you have any doubt that similar wipeouts occur regularly and without Anthropologists to unravel the approximate truth? System blindness is everywhere. We know that. And the most dangerous thing about blindness is that when we're blind, we don't know we're blind. We think we see. We take what we see as the truth, and we act.

The question remains: Is it possible to see the system story and our part in it? And if so, what difference would that "seeing" make? If the Elite could have seen their arm's length pattern *and* its effects on Mick and the rest of the system life, what other possibilities might that "see-ing" have opened up for them? Had Mick been able to see the same, how might that have shifted his experience of himself and what other strategies might that have opened up for him? It takes little imagination to recognize how such "seeing" might fundamentally reshape system life.

But how can such "seeing" happen? Anthropologists? Even in the learning environment of the Power Lab, Anthropologists walk a fine line. There is a sensitivity to their presence. Can they be trusted not to carry information from one part of the system to another? The more political the system, the more secrets there are to protect and the more sensitivity there is to "outsiders."

You might say: Couldn't Anthropologists put out clues without revealing specific data? For example, this suggestion to the Elite: *You would do well to examine your pattern of interaction and the consequences it is having for the system.* That's possible. But how do we help Mick see the Elite pattern and its consequences for him? We might put out similar clues like fortune cookie messages: *Beware of arm's length Elite.* For the Anthropologist, there is always the danger of pushing the wrong button, which then closes off access.

It occurs to me that Anthropology *is* a possibility for our systems, and its presence would move systems to an entirely new level of existence. What if a system were committed to seeing itself? Anthropologists have access to all parts of the system. Their assignment is to see the system as it is—not to interpret it or evaluate it, but simply to capture its history, as it unfolds, as objectively as they can—and then, periodically, to feed the system's story back to system members. Could we live with that? Even when we have conflicting agendas?

Let's go back to our Human Resource executive. The big secret is: Management might welcome a strike. That would give them the opportunity to shut down the plant and move closer to headquarters and a source of cheaper labor. What if that terrible secret were known? What if it were part of the system's open history? Would that destroy the system? Or would it change—greatly, I admit—the level of dialogue?

The ability to see the systems that we are a part of may be the next level of human evolution. Throughout our history, the absence of such "seeing" has resulted in endless cycles of misunderstanding, wrongful damage, abuse, oppression, and annihilation. Can we do better?

And could "Anthropology" be part of the solution?

13 Applied Anthropology: Unraveling System History

We have had but a handful of experiences in which a careful unraveling of a system's history has had a profound effect on system members. (See "Immigrant Martha Has a Breakdown" on page XX for a description of one such case.) To see such an incident, however, is to open oneself to a whole new possibility of system experience.

Because the experience is so rare, it is difficult to describe. In essence, it is like moving from a flat plane of experience to a multidimensional one—like moving from seeing a drawing of a scene to entering into the scene itself.

We are just beginning to scratch the surface in our understanding of how to make such "seeing" possible. Here are some guidelines:

1. It helps if all system members keep journals of their experiences in the system—keeping track of dates and times of significant events and recording their reactions (thoughts and feelings) to these events.

2. It helps to have an Anthropologist or a team of Anthropologists (depending on the size of the system) keeping track of system events.

3. In the unraveling process, it helps to start in the present with a TOOT. What is the picture of the current system? How are people experiencing themselves, others, and the system currently? What are the issues and dilemmas they are facing now?

4. It helps to go back to the beginning; pick a point in time and gradually work your way forward to the present. At each point, have system members review their journals, get back in touch with their experiences at the time, and then share those experiences publicly.

5. In moving toward the present, stay alert to the story that's beginning to unfold—the pieces coming together from all parts of the system. When the process works, a bright shining light is cast on the present.

In this section we have examined two types of system blindness and two strategies for seeing systems.

The TOOT helps us to avoid spatial blindness. It allows us to see into the worlds of others in the system; to see others as they are, not as our myths and prejudices define them; to understand how our different worlds impact one another; and to illuminate more productive and satisfying ways of staying in partnership with one another.

ANTHROPOLOGY helps us to avoid temporal blindness: It allows us to see our history—how we got to where we are—to see the patterns and processes developing in the system that could be blocking, frustrating, and leading us to misunderstandings and unproductive conflict. Beyond that, seeing the whole of our story deepens and enriches our experience of life.

SEEING PATTERNS OF RELATIONSHIPS

Act II

In Act One we explored the consequences of our blindness to *external* factors—our inability to see both other parts of our system and our system's history. In Act Two we will examine our *internal* blindness—our inability to see ourselves and the actions we take, without awareness or choice, that lead us out of the possibilities of partnership and into relationships of opposition, antagonism, disappointment, and warfare.

In Act Two we see human systems as constantly shifting patterns of relationship. Sometimes we are Top in a Top/Bottom relationship and sometimes we are Bottom. Sometimes we are Middle between two or more Ends pulling at us and sometimes we are one of several Ends tugging at Middle. Sometimes we are Provider supplying services to Customer and sometimes we are Customer.

For the most part, we humans do not see ourselves as being *in relationship;* we experience ourselves as autonomous entities. We do not see how powerfully this quality of *relationship* shapes our experiences of ourselves and others. In our blindness to relationship, we fall into familiar dances with one another—dances in which we become the Burdened Tops and Oppressed Bottoms, the Unsupported Ends and Torn Middles, the Judged Providers and the Righteously Done-to Customers.

The challenges are these: Can we see ourselves *in relationship?* Can we recognize the dances *while we are dancing?* Can we, from whatever side of the relationship we are in, stop the unproductive and often destructive dances and, ultimately, transform them into dances that are more satisfying and more constructive?

Two New Characters

In Act Two our stage becomes a bit more crowded. We are joined by two new characters:

She: A scientist, a student of human systems, a teacher.

He: A member of human systems and an eager learner.

14 What About All the Drama?

She says she's a scientist, a student of organization. She's been interviewing me now for several hours. I've been telling her all about this organization—about my boss, my work, our special High Zest Initiative, the meetings I had today, our new products, the current challenges. As I'm talking, I'm struck by one thing: *she's not taking any notes*. What kind of scientist is this? But I go on. I tell her the details: The battles I'm having with Charley, the various personality quirks of all the players—the bosses, the managers, the supervisors, the workers. Still no notes. I tell her about our new Instant Gratification Plan for customers. No notes. Then I review minute-by-minute all of the events of the day and the week. Then we go over the year. Still no notes. Then it's over.

"Is that all?" she says.

"That's about it," I say.

She takes out her clipboard and checks off one box.

"What's that?" I ask.

"My summary," she answers.

"Your summary?" I exclaim. "One check mark!"

"That's it," she says.

"What have you checked?" I ask.

"DBR," she says.

"DBR?"

"Yes."

"And that's all?"

"That's all."

"After all the details I gave you? All the drama. The personality sketches. The crises. The breakthroughs. That's all you have to say. DBR?" I ask incredulously.

"Yes, that covers it pretty well."

"Well, just what is this DBR?" I ask.

"It's the Dance of Blind Reflex," she says. "And thank you very much."

❏ Check here if DBR. (See definition below.)

❏ Check here if *chronic* DBR (Pattern persists throughout all seasons and despite frequent reorganizations and other shuffling of personnel.)

❏ Check here if *episodic* DBR. (Other patterns prevail, but when trouble hits, the organization falls into DBR.)

Executive Summary

In the Dance of Blind Reflex:

1. Tops are *burdened* by unmanageable complexity.

2. Bottoms are *oppressed* by insensitive higher-ups.

3. Middles are *torn*—they become weak, confused, fractionated, with no minds of their own.

4. Customers feel *done-to* (screwed) by an unresponsive system.

5. None of the players see their part in creating any of the above.

Burdened Tops

- Tops feel *burdened* by overwhelming complexity and responsibility.
- There is too much to do and not enough time to do it.
- There are fast-moving, ever-changing, unpredictable conditions to deal with.
- Tops are working with incomplete information, yet decisions need to be made. They make decisions but are not sure whether they

are the right decisions. They set priorities but are not sure that they are the right priorities.

- Tops feel a heavy responsibility for the system—so many people's fates rest in their hands.

- Tops look to Middles for support but don't feel they get the support they need. Tops can't get their initiatives down through their Middles; they can't get consistent information up from their Middles; they feel their Middles are too dependent, not entrepreneurial enough.

- Tops feel isolated and out-of-touch with much of the system.

- There are many important issues Tops know they should be dealing with—visions, missions, long-range planning, employee initiatives—but there just never seems to be the time. Tops wake regularly in the night thinking of things they should be doing.

Oppressed Bottoms

- Bottoms feel *oppressed* in the system.

- Others (higher-ups) make decisions that affect their lives in major and minor ways—reorganizations happen *to* them; initiatives come and go; health and retirement benefits are diminished; plants are closed; work forces are reduced ("they" call it "rightsizing," but Bottoms know better).

- Bottoms feel unseen and uncared for. They see things that are wrong with their situation and with the organization that higher-ups ought to be fixing but aren't.

- They feel isolated in the system; they don't have the big picture; there is no vision they can commit to; they don't see how their work fits into the whole; they don't get feedback on their work.

- Tops are invisible to them except for ceremonial acts (like Christmas visits), which seem patronizing.

- Bottoms feel that Middles add little value—they are uninformed; they may be well-meaning, but they are powerless; they are inconsistent and uneven. (Why can't those Middles get their act together?) Even Bottoms who feel central to the system's work—they are skilled, knowledgeable, experienced—feel vulnerable. Anything can happen!

- Much of Bottoms' energy is focused on "them" (higher-ups); Bottoms are angry at "them," frustrated by "them," resentful of "them," disappointed with "them."

Torn Middles

- Middles feel *torn* in the system—they feel weak, confused, and powerless.
- They are pulled between the often conflicting needs, requests, demands, and priorities of those above them and those below them.
- Middles are "loners" in the system—not connected with Tops or Bottoms, and not really connected with one another. Thus each Middle faces the stresses of the system alone, unsupported by others.
- Middles are often seen by others as confused and wishy-washy, as having no firm opinions of their own. And Middles have no independence of thought and action; they don't know who *they* are.

  Some Middles seek their identity by aligning themselves with Tops, internalizing their goals and wishes. They become more Top than Top, thereby alienating themselves from Bottoms.

  Other Middles align themselves with Bottoms, identifying with them, championing their causes, thus alienating themselves from Tops (who don't see them as sufficiently "managerial").

  Still other Middles bureaucratize themselves, creating such hurdles and hoops for others to jump over and through that others tend to avoid them as much as possible.

  Finally there are those Middles, who in trying to be fair, responsive, and even-handed with both Tops and Bottoms—and with all others who make demands on them—simply burn out in the effort.

- Middles receive little positive feedback; they are never doing quite enough for anybody. In time, many Middles internalize this feedback. ("Maybe I'm not as competent as I thought I was.")

Righteously Done-to (Screwed) Customers

- Customers feel *righteously done-to* (*screwed* is the way some put it).
- They are stunned to find that the system treats them more as problems than as opportunities.
- They feel ignored and inadequately attended to. Promises made, promises broken. Explanations. Delays. Excuses. Everything except the quality service they feel they deserve.
- Customers see the system as focused more on itself than on them.
- When Customers make what seem to them to be reasonable requests or demands, they are greeted with hostility, as if *they* are at fault.
- Sometimes frustrated Customers

  lower their standards and accept what was previously an unacceptable level of quality;

  fool themselves into believing that low-quality service really is acceptable;

  threaten to take their business elsewhere;

  do take their business elsewhere;

  get the same poor service wherever they go.
- Customers feel frustrated, angry, betrayed, powerless. DONE-TO.

How Do Those Inside the System Explain Their Condition?

Blame is freely shared:

- Bottoms blame their condition on insensitive, callous, uncaring, out-of-touch higher-ups.
- Tops blame their condition on the complexity of the world they are dealing with.
- Middles blame their condition on the demands of the middle job.
- Customers blame their condition on self-absorbed, insensitive delivery service systems.
- Everyone feels justified.
- None of the members see their own parts in creating any of this.

"So, that's all there is to my rich and complex life?" he asks. "A single check beside DBR?"

"That's it," she says.

"But my life seems so unique, so special, so beautifully chaotic."

"That's how it feels from the inside, but from the outside . . . "

"It's just DBR."

"Exactly," she says.

"Scary," he says.

16 Three Patterns of Relationship

Over the years, we have studied three patterns of relationship that occur regularly in system life, whether in the family, the classroom, the organization, or the nation. These are: Top/Bottom, Ends/Middle, and Provider/Customer.

Top/Bottom

The Top/Bottom relationship is one in which one party—Top—has designated responsibility for the system or piece of the system (the organization, division, department, classroom, meeting, project, and so forth), and the other party—Bottom—is a member within that system (worker, student, faculty member, subordinate, meeting attender, team member, and so forth).

Ends/Middle

The Ends/Middle relationship is one in which two or more parties—Ends—with their separate and sometimes conflicting agendas, look to a common party—Middle—to move their agendas ahead. Supervisors, Middle Managers, Department Chairs, Section Heads, and Negotiators regularly find themselves as Middles between two or more Ends who are looking to them for support on their agendas and priorities.

Provider/Customer

The Provider/Customer relationship is one in which one party—Provider—is designated to provide another party—Customer—with quality products or services on time and at the right price.

In each of these relationships, there is the potential for partnership in which both parties are committed to the success of their shared project or process. However, with great regularity, a dance unfolds that knocks the relationship out of the possibility of partnership. And this happens without awareness or choice. Blind reflex.

So I ask her: "How can you tell if you're a Burdened Top or an Oppressed Bottom?" And she asks me: "How are you sleeping at night?"

How can I know when I'm a Burdened Top?

When you wake in the night—
your palms are damp,
your heart is beating.
You are worrying.
You are thinking about all the people you are letting down,
about all the things you should be doing
that you're not doing,
about all the things you're not doing as well as
you should be doing.
And all the while you're lying there,
it's crystal clear to you
that everyone else is asleep.

How can I know when I'm an Oppressed Bottom?

When all your energy is focused on "Them"—
the higher-ups—
on all the things they're not doing
that they should be doing,
on all the things they're doing
that they shouldn't be doing,
your anger at Them,
your disappointment with Them,

your resentment of Them.
It's crystal clear to you
that whatever is wrong here
is *their* fault.

18 The Top/Bottom Dance of Blind Reflex

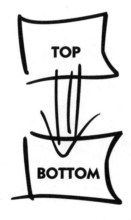

Top/Bottom

We are in a variety of Top/Bottom relationships—
sometimes as Top
and sometimes as Bottom.

We are Teacher to Student
or Student to Teacher,
Manager to Worker

or Worker to Manager,
Parent to Child
or Child to Parent,
Team Leader to Team Members
or Team Member to Team Leader,
Meeting Convener to Meeting Attender
or Meeting Attender to Meeting Convener,
Leader to Citizen
or Citizen to Leader.

We are in Top relationships
to certain system members
and in Bottom relationships
to others.
When we are in Top/Bottom relationships,
it is possible
and mutually beneficial
for us to be in partnership
regarding responsibility for the life of our system—
the classroom,
the project,
the meeting,
the team,
the family,
the nation.

However, in the Dance of Blind Reflex,
we fall out of that potential for partnership.

The DBR Top/Bottom Dance

In the Dance of Blind Reflex,
Top becomes increasingly responsible for the system—
the organization,
classroom,
department,
meeting,
team,
family,
nation—
while Bottom becomes decreasingly responsible.

As responsibility shifts to Top
and away from Bottom,
Teacher becomes responsible for the classroom,
Student not responsible;
Manager becomes responsible for the operation,
Worker not responsible;
Meeting Convener becomes responsible for the meeting,
Meeting Attender not responsible;
Parent becomes responsible for the family,
Child not responsible;
Team Leader becomes responsible for the team,
Team Member not responsible;
Leader becomes responsible for the nation,
Citizen not responsible.

And these shifts happen
without awareness or choice
by either Top
or Bottom.

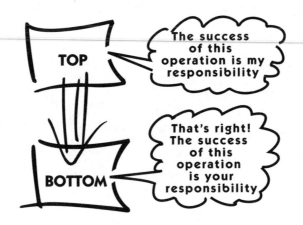

The Burdened and the Oppressed

And so it is plain to see how,
when difficulties arise,
Top falls into *burden*—
"There are all of these issues I should be handling because
I'm Top;
I can't handle them all;
I'm not handling them well;
others are counting on me"—
while Bottom falls into *oppression*—
"Look at all these problems They are not taking care of;
They sure are either malicious, insensitive, or incompetent."

Stepping out of the Dance of Blind Reflex

Despite its bad reputation,
awareness *is* everything
(or almost everything).

Seeing the dance gives choice:
to continue the dance
or to change it.

As Top
we can see ourselves
pulling responsibility
up to ourselves
and away from others,
and we can see Bottoms
turning it over
to us.

As Bottom
we can see ourselves
giving responsibility up to Tops,
and we can see them
pulling it up to themselves.

As Top
we can choose
to stop sucking it up to ourselves,
and instead
find ways of creating responsibility in others
while remaining responsible ourselves.

As Bottom
we can choose
to stop holding Them wholly responsible for the system,
and instead
see ourselves as central players
in the success of this classroom,
department,

organization,

meeting,

family,

team,

nation.

Resistance

Some Tops complain about their burden
while clinging to it.
They fear losing control
when they are still responsible
(a not unreasonable fear);
they fear that others won't be as responsible
or as skilled
or as committed as they are.
They are concerned that creating responsibility in others—
involving them,
training them,
developing them—
takes too much time.
It is easier to simply do it yourself.
And some Tops simply accept burden
as being part of the job.

With awareness comes choice,
and some Tops choose burden.

And some Bottoms complain about their oppression
while clinging to it.
They complain about the insensitivity
and incompetence

of Tops,
and about the negative consequences these have
for the classroom,
team,
organization,
department,
meeting,
family,
nation,
but refuse to accept their roles as central players
in the success
or failure
of the system.
"Why should I? I'm just a Bottom."
"They get paid to take the heat."

With awareness comes choice,
and some Bottoms choose oppression.

Partners in Creation

In the Dance of Blind Reflex,
Tops are the creators of the system,
and Bottoms are the recipients
(or victims) of it.

The challenge in stepping out of the Dance
is for Tops and Bottoms—
each side bringing its unique
experiences,
knowledge,
and skills—

to become co-creators of the system—

the classroom,

the team,

the department,

the organization,

the meeting,

the family,

the nation,

the world;

sharing responsibility

for its successes

and its failures

in each moment

and in the long term.

■

He: That *is* a beautiful dance, isn't it?

She: How do you mean?

He: It all fits so nicely together. The more Top plays Top, the easier it is for Bottom to play Bottom. And vice versa.

She: Exactly. And what makes it especially compelling is that neither party realizes it is *doing* anything. It's all blind reflex. Top is burdened, Bottom is oppressed, and that's the way it is. No one does anything. It's simply the way things are. Or so it seems.

He: So how do we avoid the dance?

She: First, we see it.

He: And then?

She: And then we choose: Continue the dance or try a new dance.

He: That seems straightforward.

She: We shall see.

19 It Takes Two to Tango . . . or Does It?

She has a conversation with Top and Bottom:

Bottom: I'd assume responsibility if Top would let it go.

Top: I'd let it go if Bottom would take it on.

Bottom: I'd do my part if only Top would do its.

Top: Everyone knows: You can't make someone responsible.

Top and Bottom: It takes two to tango; that's obvious.

She: If the two agreed, that would be nice. It would make for change smooth and easy.

Top and Bottom: That's what it takes.

She: But what if only one chooses to change the dance?

Top and Bottom: Sorry, it can't be done.

She: Are you sure?

Top and Bottom: It takes two to tango. First principle.

She: What if you began to change the dance yourself?

Top: You'd look damn silly.

Bottom: You'd be left out there dancing all by yourself.

She: And if you kept on dancing?

Bottom: You might get put away.

Top: Or fired.

Bottom: Or yelled at.

She: Is that all?

Top: I suppose, after a while, you might just give up and go back to the old dance.

She: That's possible. Anything else?

Bottom: It's possible that the relationship would just end. The two could no longer work together.

She: That's also possible. Is there anything else?

Top: (reluctantly) I suppose it's also possible that, in time, the other might choose to join you in the new dance.

She: So that's possible too.

Top and Bottom: So everything's possible. Big deal!

She: Precisely! It is a big deal. Don't you see what you just said?

Top and Bottom: No!

She: When you change the dance, you create possibility—no more, no less. You break the pattern. Everything is up for grabs. The relationship, as it has been, can no longer continue. So now what? You create chaos—a disruption of the energy pattern.

Top: That's a good thing?

She: Good or bad, it's what happens when one chooses to change the dance.

Bottom: It sounds like a mess.

She: So, you'd prefer something neater—an organized transformation, complete with predictable outcomes?

Top: Who wouldn't?

She: Then, when the other says "No" to the new dance, you stop. Is that it?

Bottom: It's only sensible.

She: It's not sensible; it's an excuse. "No" is not the end of the process; it is the beginning. It is the sign that the relationship is entering the messy zone of possibility. If you quit, you miss the opening. It is exactly as you have said: If you continue to dance the new dance alone everything is possible, and when everything is possible, things are a mess: They may put you away; the relationship might end; you might fall back into the old dance; the other might choose to join you in creating a new dance. This is the mess of transformation. Can it be any other way? Think of relationship as energy—settled into a particular pattern, uncomfortable for all parties, yet comfortable in its predictability. And now you disrupt the pattern. Why would you expect that to be a smooth and predictable process? You have created flux, instability. In that instability lies hope—the hope of creating new patterns that will be more satisfactory for all. Don't run away from flux. Work with it. It is the sound of the old dance shaking.

What is power after all?
Power is the ability to act as if you can make happen
whatever it is you want to make happen,
knowing that you cannot
and being willing to work with whatever does
happen.

20 Let's Declare Bankruptcy: Transforming the Top/Bottom Dance

When the Dance of Blind Reflex is all there is, it remains invisible to us. It is only when some variation or mutation occurs that one is able to see both the regular pattern and its alternative.

Such a mutation in the Top/Bottom pattern occurred in one of our Organization Workshop exercises. A familiar story was unfolding: Tops were overwhelmed by demands coming at them from Customers, from their Managers, and from Workers. The time pressures were excruciating. The organization was in disarray. There was little patience to be found anywhere. Customers were dissatisfied—seeing the organization as inadequately responsive to their needs. Money was not coming in; consequently, there were few funds for salaries. And Worker complaints were mounting. None of this was unusual given the complexity of the conditions; but it was what happened next that opened our eyes both to the usual pattern and to the possibility of transformation.

The Tops were meeting in their office. It was painfully clear that the organization was failing. One Top suggested the possibility of declaring bankruptcy. "It's hopeless. There's no point in going on." There was general agreement. Bankruptcy could end this nightmare. "Let's go out there and finish this."

It was at this point that the pattern began to disintegrate—first at the Top, then at the Bottom.

As the Tops were leaving to make their announcement, one Top stopped them. "Why are *we* deciding this?" he asked. The others were stunned. The question was too far out of the pattern even to be understood at first. The Top persisted. "Why is it *our* decision? Why don't we tell the others the situation and see what they say?"

Even if one did not understand the language, one could see and feel the discombobulation at the top. Confusion. Heated conversation. Conflicting statements—sometimes coming from the same mouth.

"Why are we talking about this?"
"Why not?"
"It's already settled."
"Maybe."
"It's our decision."
"Is it?"

After considerable back and forth it was agreed: "What's our rush? Let's put the situation to the others and see what happens. What's to lose?"

And so they did. And then the discombobulation at the Bottom:

"You Tops screwed up."
"What can we do?"
"I guess it's over."
"Is it?"

"Why bother us with this; it's your business."

"It's *our* business."

"It's hopeless."

"We can fix it."

"It's dead."

"Not yet it isn't."

"Now what?"

"Let's stop."

"Let's go on."

A messy time. Confusing. "What are we to do? The past is no guide for us." Out of the mess a new form emerged. The organization wasn't dead. There was no bankruptcy. There was a shift in energy throughout the organization and among its Customers. There was new commitment to make this thing work. A culture change. Projects were completed; money came in; salaries were paid. Not everyone was swept up in this culture change. Some Workers remained committed to their traditional Bottomness—whining, complaining, feeling put-upon, more committed to holding Tops responsible than to success—just as there was some feeling at the Top that involvement of the Workers—although it saved the organization—was an admission of Top failure.

And so we step back from the event. What happened here? The mutation reveals quite clearly both the pattern and its alternative. The *Big Issue* hits. It's crystal clear to Top that Top decides. Just as it's equally clear to Bottom that Top decides (assuming Bottom ever hears about the issue, which, itself, is unlikely until it is too late to do anything about it). Then the mutation. The shift that fundamentally transforms our world: Can we be in partnership around the life of this system?

Partnership may be a much abused term, but isn't that what we are talking about? Even though we are in a Top/Bottom relationship, isn't it in our mutual interest to be in partnership about the life of this system? this organization? this classroom? this project? this meeting? wherever we are prone to falling into the traditional pattern? And if we are truly in partnership over the life of this system, haven't we fundamentally transformed this Top/Bottom relationship?

He: It seems to me you're talking about a lot more than just life in the organization. This Top/Bottom stuff is everywhere—the community, the government, the world.

She: Isn't it.

He: When I think about being Bottom, it strikes me as a painfully comfortable place.

She: That's an interesting phrase—"painfully comfortable."

He: But that's just what it is. I have all of my complaints about "Them"—the mayor, the city government, the president, the world leaders—all these things that they're doing wrong, all the aggravation they're causing me. At the same time there's something very comfortable about having them to blame.

She: It would be quite a project to turn that around, wouldn't it?

21 The Universal Civics Course

This business of trusting or not trusting Tops is truly a phony issue. It's as if the issue is about *their* trustworthiness. But the issue of system membership is not about "Them," it is about "Us." How trustworthy are we as members and citizens? Are we, even as lowly members, willing to accept our roles as co-creators of our systems? When we say *I trust and support the Tops,* isn't that an easy way to step away from our responsibility for this system? Isn't that simply a prelude to our blaming "Them" when the system fails?

When the leaders' grand visions turn to ashes—as they so often do—we kick the bums out, impeach them, send them into exile, hang them, or shoot them. And then we wait. We wait for the next leader whom we can again hold responsible for our lives and our systems. And on and on it goes.

There are two parallel myths about leaders: The first is that all progress comes from the actions of enlightened leaders; the second is that all the horrors of humanity—warfare, oppression, genocide—are attributable to demonic leadership.

These myths are comforting to us as system members in that they absolve us of responsibility for both progress and disaster. However, they do not reflect historical truth. The eight-hour workday was not arrived at because factory owners thought it would be a nice thing to do. The advance of women was not the result of men deciding it was high time to give the ladies a fair shake. Nor did the end of slavery happen because slaveholders and the Government decided that freedom was a legitimate right of all people. In all cases, progress occurred not out of the benevolence and wisdom of leaders, but out of the messy, impudent, and relentless pushback—through strikes, demonstrations, resistance, and civil disobedience—of system members.

And it also is true that oppression, warfare, and holocausts have existed only through the acquiescence of the members.

Which brings us to the Universal Civics Course.

---

civics *n:* the study of government and of the rights and duties of citizens

The rights and duties of citizens: Now there's an interesting idea!

I propose that we develop a Universal Civics Course. Its purpose will be to enlighten all of us regarding our rights and duties as members/citizens.

In the course, we will explore the role not only of the leaders but also of the members in humankind's history of warfare, oppression, and genocide: How the members trusted too much. How they abandoned their own responsibility. How they were too lazy to work at citizenship. How they went for the bait when their leaders told them how special and noble and deserving they were in contrast to the others, in contrast to "Them." How they found easy targets for their frustrations. How they continued living the good life for themselves while others were surrounded by evil and injustice. How they fought with one another instead of pushing back at the leaders.

We will study case after case—from the past and the present—of this pattern of member complicity in evil. And then the first phase of the course will end.

The Final Examination

Some years later, the Leader will call our graduates out to war. "Our cause is noble," the Leader will say. "We want nothing for ourselves, only justice for others. The enemy is the Devil, set on our destruction," he will say. "Our people are great. We have not started this war, nor do we want it. But our personal wishes must be set aside in the face of this great threat. To war, boys and girls, to war! Our cause is just!"

Our graduates will listen to the Leader. They will study the facts. They will dig deep—behind the propaganda. They will observe the Leader closely: They will see all the tricks he uses to arouse their emotions and dampen their minds. ("Notice that chill that runs up and down your spine. Isn't it great how he does that?") They have seen all of this before. They will study, observe, discuss, and when the leader speaks, they will listen hard.

Then they will look at one another; smiles will break out across their faces; there will be giggles, then laughter, then wave after wave of bent-over-double, helpless, uncontrollable laughter.

And then the difficult business of co-creation will begin. Which is the final examination for the Universal Civics Course.

Who Wants the Universal Civics Course?

Does anyone in power want the Universal Civics Course? Think about it. You're the owner of your business or the Top Executive of your company or the parent in the family or the teacher in the classroom or the Leader of the nation. Do you want your members to be co-creators? How can I even begin to create the Universal Civics Course if my students insist on being co-creators? Wouldn't we much prefer that our members trust us to do the right thing?

It is naive to expect leaders to encourage the development of the Universal Civics Course. Maybe that's the way it should be. The rights and duties of citizens is members business.

**A**nd sometimes

we are in Ends/Middle relationships:

Sometimes as Middle between two or more Ends,

who look to us for support on their separate agendas;

and sometimes as an End

looking to the Middle for support on our agenda.

And when we are blind to this relationship,

we are in danger of falling into the dance of

the Unsupported End

and the Torn Middle.

Ends/Middle

In the Ends/Middle relationship,
two or more parties—Ends—
with their separate and sometimes conflicting agendas
are looking to a common party, Middle,
to move their separate agendas ahead.

In organization life
we are in a variety of Ends/Middle relationships:
Sometimes as an End
and sometimes as a Middle.

Some of our Ends/Middle relationships are *vertical:*

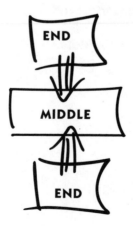

We are Supervisors between Workers
and Managers;
we are Department Chairs
between Faculty
and Administration.

Other Ends/Middle relationships are *horizontal:*

We are Negotiators between
one party
and another;
we are Managers
between Customers
and Producers.

And some Ends/Middle relationships are *group-to-group:*

We are the Procurement organization
between Suppliers
and Manufacturers.

In Ends/Middle relationships,
it is possible and mutually beneficial for us to function in
partnership,
in moving ahead Ends' agendas.

In the Dance of Blind Reflex, however,
we fall out of that potential for partnership.

The Ends/Middle Dance of Blind Reflex

In the Ends/Middle Dance of Blind Reflex
Ends become decreasingly responsible
for resolving their own issues and conflicts,
while Middle becomes increasingly responsible
for resolving these.

And this happens without the awareness
of either Ends
or Middle.

As this shift occurs,
Ends make demands on Middle,
which seem simple enough to the Ends
("Any competent Middle should be able to handle this"),
but which Middle finds most difficult to meet
while still feeling responsible for meeting them.

The Unsupported and the Torn

It is plain to see
how Ends fall into being the *Unsupported*

("Why am I stuck with such a weak and ineffectual
Middle?"),
while Middle falls into being the *Torn*
("My work is important—I am needed by both sides—but I
can't seem to please anyone. Maybe I *am* weak . . .
confused . . . ineffective . . . incompetent").

Stepping Out of the Dance

With awareness comes the possibility of choice.

As Ends we can become aware—
we can see ourselves
shifting responsibility
for resolving issues and conflicts
from ourselves
to Middle.
We can see ourselves
holding Middle responsible
for accomplishments
we would find difficult if not impossible for ourselves.

As Middles we can become aware—
we can see ourselves
taking on full responsibility
for resolving Ends' issues and conflicts.

As Middles we need to find ways
of involving Ends more directly
in resolving *their* own issues and conflicts.

As Ends we need to become more directly involved
in resolving our own issues and conflicts.

Resistance

Some Middles,
while complaining about the condition of being torn,
cling to it.
They enjoy being in the middle—
needed by both sides—
so central,
so important.
("What would I be if I weren't in the middle?")

And some Ends,
while complaining about the condition of being unsupported,
cling to it.
It's nice not having to do those difficult things oneself;
it's nice having Middle to blame when things go wrong.

With awareness comes choice:
What do we want?
Importance?
Ease?
Someone to blame?
Or
Moving one's agenda ahead?

It's our choice.

Partners in Conflict Resolution

In the Dance of Blind Reflex
Middles are responsible
for resolving Ends' issues and conflicts;
Ends are not.
The challenge in stepping out of the dance

is for each party to bring its unique resources to bear.

Ends are the central players;

it is their issues that need to be resolved,

their agendas that need to be moved ahead.

To this process, Middle brings its own unique perspective—

not the perspective of one End

or the other—

but Middle's own view.

And Middle brings tools

that support Ends

in working out their issues.

■

He: This is gonna be tough. *They want me in the middle!*

She: First, be clear that your job is to help *them* resolve *their* issues and conflicts.

He: Why do they need me?

She: To use your skills and your perspective to help *them* deal with the issues *they* are facing.

He: They want *me* to do it for them.

She: And your job is to get them in partnership around resolving their own issues.

He: Partnership again! It's getting clearer to me that this partnership business you keep talking about is a most unnatural act.

She: There's always the dance to fall back on. And keep in mind that you're not the one who is always in the middle. Sometimes you're the End who is making unreasonable demands of Middle. So think about partnership from that angle.

He: Oh!

Sometimes the pain of the dance becomes so excruciating for one party that it leads that party to unilaterally break out of the dance into the *possibility* of transformation. Such was the case with Daniel.

Daniel had been a Middle in one of our Power Labs. The Ends/Middle dance had been going on vigorously for several days. Tops and Bottoms had been holding Daniel responsible for resolving their own issues, and Daniel had been pulling that responsibility into himself. Both Tops and Bottoms were dissatisfied with Daniel's performance: To the Bottoms, he was too weak, wishy-washy, a mindless lackey of the Tops; and to the Tops, he was indecisive, lacking a "managerial mentality." Despite the abuse and lack of support from both sides, Daniel persisted: Working morning to night, committed to keeping this system from falling apart, feeling that this was *his* responsibility.

Then something snapped. Without warning Daniel dropped out of the society. He stopped caring about the Tops and Bottoms. He spent his days by the pool reading. He resisted all efforts to bring him back into the society—into the middle. He never did reenter. And, despite others' jabs at him as a dropout ("What lesson do you learn from this, Daniel?"), he felt terrific.

But this is only part one of the story. When Daniel returned to his "back-home" job, he immediately found himself right back in the middle. His Bottoms were unhappy about some new arrangements made by his Tops. The Bottoms wanted Daniel to come down, hear their complaints, and then fix it up with the Tops. For that is how the dance usually went—with Daniel in the middle between the Tops (as one End) and the Bottoms (as the other); with Daniel feeling very important and central to the situation, carrying messages from one End to the other, explaining one side to the other, never doing quite enough for either side, and so forth. But something popped and the dance was interrupted and the possibility of transformation began to unfold, first for Daniel, then in his interactions with Bottoms and, then, Tops, and finally in their interactions with one another.

We do not know Daniel's precise thoughts when he was first approached by the Bottoms, but we suspect it was something like the following: *"This is not* my *problem"* (A very important first step). *"This is* their *problem. What I need to do is help* them *work this out with* one another."

So Daniel went to the Bottoms and listened to their issues; but when they instructed him to carry their message to the Tops, he refused. He told them what he would do was set up a meeting between them and the Tops so that they could present their issues directly. He said he would work with them, coach them, support them in making the best case they could, but he made it clear that he would not *do it* for them. So now the usual dance began to unravel.

"No, Daniel, you do it."
"Sorry, it's your issue, not mine."
"But you're our Middle; it's your job."
"No, my job is to help you do what you feel needs to be done, but you've got to do it."

Is this resistance? Should Daniel stop because the Bottoms said "No" to his proposal? Or is "No" precisely what one should expect—possibly even look forward to—as the energy pattern of the familiar dance is disrupted.

Daniel persisted, and the Bottoms finally agreed that, with Daniel's coaching, they would take their case to the Tops.

A parallel process occurred when Daniel brought this proposal for a face-to-face meeting to the Tops.

The sounds of the dance breaking up:

"We're too busy."

"It's important that you hear directly from them."

"That's what we hired you to do."

"You hired me to use my best judgment."

When the Top says "No," is it the end of the conversation or the beginning? Or is "No" simply the sound of the familiar dance shaking?

For Daniel, "No" was the beginning of the conversation; he persisted, and the Tops agreed to the meeting.

Daniel coached the Bottoms. The meeting was held. It was awkward at first but quickly developed into a productive encounter. Tops and Bottoms worked out a satisfactory resolution of their issues. Both sides felt it was a good meeting. Daniel commented that he had "the driest palms in the room" (palmar perspiration count may be an objective measure of where responsibility lies).

The shift was toward partnership. *Middle did not abdicate responsibility.* Daniel remained committed to the resolution of this issue, but what he made clear to himself and others was that this was not his issue but theirs and that both Ends must be in full partnership around its resolution.

Some might see this shift as diminishing the role of Middle. This is clearly not the case. For Daniel, it opened up a whole new realm of possibility about what it meant to be Middle. "I began to look around and ask myself: 'What's not happening that could be happening? Who are the people who need to be together to make it happen? How can I get them together and support their interaction with one another?'"

Yet, even after this highly productive meeting between Daniel's Tops and Bottoms, there were lingering pressures to restore the old dance. Immediately following the meeting, when all the others had left the room, the Top of the Tops said to Daniel: "Great meeting, Daniel." And then, after a pause, "But don't you ever do it again."

So for Daniel—and for all the rest of us Daniels out there—is "No" no, or is it the continuing echo of the traditional Ends/Middle dance shaking?

24 Organizations in the Middle

The Ends/Middle dance is not limited to interactions among individuals. It also takes place among organizational groups. Take, for example, the situation faced by a worldwide Procurement organization. Their job was to purchase parts and equipment from Suppliers for use by Manufacturing. There was considerable confusion within Procurement as to what their role was, and there were constant complaints from both Suppliers and Manufacturing.

Manufacturing was constantly after Procurement to reduce costs. ("We're under pressure to keep our costs down. You [Procurement] account for over 60 percent of our costs. Do better!")

And the Suppliers felt vulnerable. They wanted long-term relationships with the company and were willing to meet all sorts of price and process demands to make that possible. Suppliers were constantly adjusting but still felt vulnerable.

Procurement felt that Manufacturing was difficult to deal with; they made unreasonable demands and were unwilling to get involved in what they thought were Procurement's problems.

Once the Director of Procurement saw that the department was caught up in a classical Ends/Middle dance, the choice became clear: We can continue to assume *full* responsibility for procurement or we can work to move some of that responsibility out to Manufacturing and the Suppliers.

The decision was made to change the role of Procurement from *doing* procurement to *facilitating* the procurement relationship between Supplier and Manufacturing.

There was initial resistance from Manufacturing ("Procurement is your job") and from some people within Procurement, as *facilitating* procurement seemed less powerful and less significant than *doing* procurement (despite the aggravation that regularly accompanied the doing).

Is resistance resistance or merely the sound of the old dance shaking? The Director persisted. "Responsibility is now where it belongs. Our business is to put Suppliers and Manufacturing together. That's where the issues of Supplier security and Manufacturing costs are best handled."

nd sometimes

we are in Provider/Customer relationships:

sometimes as Provider

and sometimes as Customer.

And when we are blind to this relationship,

we are in danger of falling into the dance of

the Judged Provider

and the Done-to Customer.

25 The Provider/Customer Dance of Blind Reflex

Provider/Customer

In organization life,
we are in a variety of Provider/Customer relationships:
Sometimes as Provider
designated to provide some service or product to another
person or group,
and sometimes as Customer—
the supposed recipient of some high-quality product or
service from the Provider.

When we are in Provider/Customer relationships,
it is possible
and mutually beneficial
for us to be in partnership
regarding the delivery of high-quality products and services.

In the Dance of Blind Reflex, however,
we regularly fall out of that potential for partnership.

The Provider/Customer Dance of Blind Reflex

In the Dance of Blind Reflex,
Provider becomes increasingly responsible

for the delivery of the product or service,
and Customer becomes decreasingly responsible.

As responsibility shifts,
delivery becomes the Provider's business
and entitlement becomes the Customer's.
And this happens without awareness
of either Provider
or Customer.

■

He: Wait a minute! Stop the dance. There's something seriously wrong here.

She: What's wrong?

He: Look, I had no problem seeing the Top/Bottom shift. The Ends/Middle shift caused me a little more difficulty. *But this!* This is going too far. Customers *are* entitled. That's what it is to be Customer.

She: So what happens when the Customer gets unsatisfactory delivery?

He: *The Customer's not supposed to get unsatisfactory delivery!*

She: Right. But what happens when it comes anyway?

He: I suppose you get mad, you complain, and you might even find yourself another supplier.

She: Exactly. And what don't you get?

He: (pondering) I guess the thing you don't get is delivery.

She: Exactly. You get anger, you get frustration, and you get a solid dose of righteous indignation. What you don't get is delivery. So the question is: What matters more to you? Delivery or righteous indignation?

He: (whining) But it's the Provider's fault!

She: I guess your answer is righteous indignation.

The Done-to (Screwed) and the Judged

And so it is plain to see how,
when quality delivery fails to materialize,
Customer falls into being the Done-to (Screwed):
"Look at this poor delivery!
It's your fault.
I'm the Customer;
I deserve better."
And Provider falls into being the Judged:
"We did the best we could.
The Customers make unreasonable demands;
they are fickle, disloyal.
They don't know what's good for them;
they don't understand our constraints;
they don't appreciate what a fine job we've done."

Partners in Delivery

It is possible
and desirable
for Provider
and Customer
to be in partnership in the delivery process.
Customer needs to share responsibility for the delivery
process.
("If I don't get what I want, then I'm also to blame.")
Customer needs to become more directly involved in the
delivery process—
knowing how the delivery system works;
setting clear demands and standards;
getting into the delivery process early as a partner,
not late as a judge;
staying close to the Provider.
And the Provider needs to allow the Customer into the
delivery process.

∎

He: You can bet there'll be resistance on this one. Does the Customer want to be responsible? Does the Supplier want the Customer messing around in the Provider's business?

She: There will be resistance, which is why we have so much poor delivery and so many Righteously Screwed Customers and Judged Providers. But is resistance just resistance? Isn't it also the sound of the old dance breaking up? Isn't it also the harbinger of the possibility of transformation?

He: Or else it's the Dance of Blind Reflex.

She: Exactly.

26 Overcontrol or Transformation: The Mutant Customer

There is much talk about the need for "paradigm shifts"—fundamentally different models for comprehending human behavior in social systems. It is difficult, however, to recognize such shifts, even when they are directly in front of us. The difficulty is this: We view the new through the old lens and, as a consequence, we look without seeing. Consider the following example from the Organization Workshop.

The usual Customer pattern is unfolding. The Customers, having made their presentations to Tops regarding their needs and requirements, are now waiting patiently in their offices for results. They sit and wait.

Not all Customers are waiting, however. Sandra is making quite a pain in the neck of herself. She is constantly at the Tops' office making new demands. The Tops keep assuring her that her project is in good hands and well underway, but that's not good enough for Sandra. She wants more involvement. The Tops see her as an interference. Sandra wants to have some say in who works on her project. She wants to meet directly with the Workers. She is not satisfied simply getting progress reports from Middles or Tops. She insists on being right in there with the Workers.

Sandra is looking a bit strange to the other Customers—pushy, lacking in trust. Apparently Sandra cares little for the other Customers' reactions; she persists. The Tops try to hold her off, but Sandra is not to be stopped. In the end she gets her way: She meets the Workers; she is involved in selecting the team to work on her project; she engages directly with the team, meeting regularly with team members.

Program staff have observed all of this: Sandra's "pushiness"; the discomfort she is producing in Tops and Middles; her unrelenting drive for involvement. One staff member comments: "That's Sandra with her inordinate needs for control." Other staff nod in agreement. It's clear to all that that's what they're dealing with here—an inordinate need for control.

There are other results that indicate that something beyond "control needs" is going on here. Other Customers complain about the service they get: Promises are made but not kept; delivery is late; products are substandard. It is clear to these Customers that the organization has failed *them*. Sandra, however, is delighted with her results: She gets surprisingly good products; she enjoys interacting directly with the Workers; and they enjoy her. It seems that only management and the staff have problems with Sandra.

What has Sandra done? She changed the dance and in doing so caused the predictable chaos. The other Customers and the Organization were dancing comfortably with one another. [Organization: "We are responsible for delivery; you are not." Customers: "You are responsible for delivery; we are not." And when the dance ends, the Organization feels unfairly judged while the Customers feel righteously screwed.]

Sandra, by contrast, chose to create a different dance: "I am also responsible for delivery." And she continued that dance in the face of resistance, until in the end, the Organization reluctantly joined in with her.

Through one set of lenses, we see a pattern of personal behavior: Pushiness, overcontrol, lack of trust, and so forth. Through another set of lenses, we see one person transforming the predictable Provider/Customer dance.

■

He: Hmm!

She: What is it?

He: I'm beginning to see another side to this.

She: And?

He: I'm often in a service role in my organization. Doesn't that put me into a Provider/Customer relationship with my clients?

She: It sure does.

He: And that's what I'm wondering about. Am I the Provider sucking up all the responsibility for service? And are my Customers pushing all the responsibility for service onto me? And am I letting that happen?

She: It's hard not to, isn't it?

He: I think it is happening.

She: Ah, the Space of Service. It's a mine field!

94

27 Abused and Misused in the Space of Service

The Service Provider Enters the Space of Service

I am the Service Provider—
the staff specialist,
the technical advisor,
the consultant,
the field service specialist,
the Human Resources resource,
the therapist.
I enter the Space of Service.
I have my expertise.
I know much about that
but little about this particular situation.
What's unique here?
Where are the minefields?
Whose agendas am I serving?
Whose agendas are being ignored?
What are people looking for?
Instant solutions?
Painless solutions?
Are some skeptical,
others hopeful,
still others hopeless?
Whatever,
they all look to me.

The Service Provider Needs to Be of Immediate Value

I am the Service Provider.
I enter the Space of Service.
It is crystal clear to me:
I must be of immediate value.
It is crystal clear to my clients:
I must be of immediate value.

The Service Provider Becomes the Expert

I am the Service Provider.
I must be of immediate value.
I am the *expert;*
I have the solution to your problem,
the system to fix your system,
the process,
the theory,
the tools.
I am the answer to your prayers.

Or . . .

The Service Provider Becomes the Servant

I am the Service Provider.
I must be of immediate value.
I am your *servant;*
whatever you ask, I do.

The help you request
is the help I give;
the solution you seek
is the solution you receive.
And I clean ashtrays, too.

The Service Provider "Experts" and "Servants"

I expert you,
I servant you.
The more I expert
and the more I servant,
the less I illuminate,
the more I confuse.
What does your system need?
Really need?

The Service Provider is Abused and Misused

I am the Service Provider.
Expert or servant,
I come away unclean—
abused,
misused,
of no real value,
my true expertise untapped,
your real needs unaddressed.
I took you and your system
where *I* wanted to go
or where *you* wanted to go
and not where *it* needed to go.

The Service Provider Takes a Stand

I am the Service Provider,
and you are the Client.
My stand is to be
of real and lasting value to this system,
so that it will be a more empowered system
after I am gone.
I have no instant solution.
Can you handle that?
Can I?
I have my expertise,
and you have yours.
Let us use our expertise.
Let us learn together
to understand this system,
appreciate its possibilities,
strengthen it,
move it ahead
in partnership.

■

He: This makes sense to me. I don't enjoy being the servant and I
don't like being the expert and I do like the idea of being in partnership with my clients, being committed to learning together,
being committed to providing the best service possible. But . . .

She: But they won't like it?

He: Exactly.

She: And they'll resist. They might say "No." They might threaten to
take their business elsewhere. In fact, they just might do that—find
themselves some other willing expert or servant. Or you and they
might just fall back into the old dance. Or you might succeed in
transforming the dance. It's all possible.

He: It certainly will stir things up.

She: Transformation always does. Always. You are rearranging the energy.

He: The sound of the old dance shaking.

She: Exactly.

28 The Web of Relationships

He: What I'm beginning to see is that my life is a web of patterns of relationships.

Sometimes I'm Top

and sometimes I'm Bottom.

Sometimes I'm in the middle between Ends

and sometimes I'm an End.

Sometimes I'm the Provider

and sometimes I'm the Customer.

And all of these may be going on simultaneously.

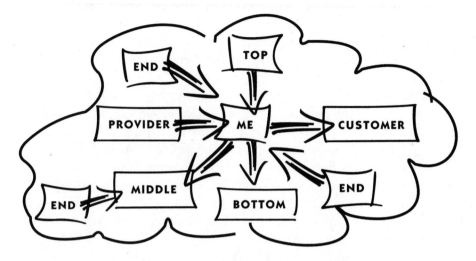

She: And in each relationship, there is the lure of the Dance of Blind Reflex.

He: One party takes on all responsibility for the process, while the other lets it go. It's all so neat.

She: And blind.

He: Partnership . . . it's such an unnatural act.

29 How to Clean Sidewalks

Skill-training has its place, but what we are exploring here has less to do with skill than with something much more elusive, something that, for the point of this discussion, I'll call "being."

Skill-training has to do with "doing"—how to do this and how to do that. So let me be clear: I strongly recommend skill-training. If you are to spend time in meetings, it can be very useful to develop greater meeting skills. The same holds true for handling conflicts, dealing with difficult people, brainstorming, problem solving, and myriad other things one must do in order to survive and thrive in systems.

There are, however, many situations in which skill—how to do—is less to the point than being—how to be. Let me take a hypothetical case.

Let us say I am the youngest in the family; my brother is the oldest. Let us say that the two of us live on similar urban streets but in different cities. And let us say that both of us are troubled by—in fact, incensed over—the huge amounts of dog droppings that litter our sidewalks and sometimes find their way to the bottoms of our shoes. And let us say that both of us have spent considerable time whining and complaining about those inconsiderate dog owners who allow their pets to indiscriminately foul our sidewalks. And let us say that, coincidentally, on the same day, my brother and I separately experience epiphanies regarding the dog droppings. Suddenly, it strikes each of us separately that we have been Bottom in the matter of dog droppings. And it strikes us that, rather than continue to be victims of this problem, we could be central to making it go away. For both of us, this is a liberating and exhilarating thought.

My brother, the first born, has proclivities to leadership. I, the last born, tend to do things myself. My brother organizes the neighborhood; I go out and buy a huge broom. We both succeed. He and his neighbors work out their methods; I delight in going out periodically with my broom. (Neighbors across the street mistakenly assume I was hired to do the job, so they hire their own dog dropping technician.) Both my brother and I are delighted in our power, in our abilities to convert this complaint into an accomplishment.

Is there a skill to this? Should I learn about community organizing or should my brother learn about broom pushing? I think not. In this, as in so many other cases, we are dealing less with doing than with being. Once the shift in being occurs, we manage to find our way to doing. On the other hand, unless there is a shift in being, all the skill-training in the world will not help.

Before leaving this section, we want to explore another system relationship and another dance. We dance this dance within our organizations and in many other contexts. This is the dance of the Dominant and the Dominated, through which we fall out of the possibility of partnership with one another and into misunderstanding, antagonism, oppression, and destruction.

30 Dominant/Dominated

The other side of dominant is not submissive;
it is dominated.

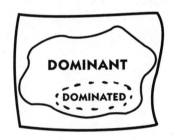

The Dominant and the Dominated

In many systems,
there are two cultures:
the Dominant
and the Dominated.

The Dominated exist within the Dominant culture:
females in a male dominated society,
acquired companies within the acquiring company,
people of color in a white dominated society,
homosexuals in a heterosexual dominated society,
Native Americans in America,
Soviet states in a Russian-dominated empire,
Palestinians in Israel,
Blacks in South Africa,
French-Canadians in English-Canadian-dominated society,
Serbs in the Ottoman Empire,
Jews in anti-Semitic societies,
Catholic, Japanese, Chinese, and other early immigrants in
the U.S.A.
The Dominated
within the Dominant.

■

He: So we're not talking about "minorities"?
She: Absolutely right. Minority, majority—that's not the issue. The
question is: Who are the Dominant? And who are the Dominated?

The Dominant Culture

The Dominants' culture
is invisible to them;
it is the water in which they swim,
the air they breathe.
To the Dominants,
how they speak
is the way one speaks,

how they dress
is how one dresses,
their values
are *the* values,
their history
is *the* history.

To the Dominants,
the culture of the Dominated
is not merely different,
it is wrong—
wrong speech,
wrong dress,
wrong emotionality,
wrong spirituality,
wrong values.

The culture of the Dominated is seen as strange,
sometimes comical,
usually lesser,
inferior.

The Survival of the Dominated

To the Dominated,
the culture of the Dominants
is oppressive—
there is no space for *their* voice,
their dress,
their values,
their history.

How to survive as a Dominated
within the Dominant culture?

Adopt.
We can suppress our culture
and adopt their culture,
become more like them:
white-ish Blacks,
man-ish women,
Gentile-ish Jews,
straight-ish gays.
We can walk like them,
talk like them,
dress like them,
think like them.
We can make our way
as best we can
as one of them
in their world.

Embrace.
We can accept our fate—
the Dominated within the Dominant.
This is our life;
we can choose it,
love it,
embrace it,
and make our way
as best we can.

Separate.
We can separate from them—
from their businesses,

their schools,
their churches,
their government.
We can reject their ways
and elaborate our ways,
our culture;
create our own businesses,
churches,
schools,
government.
We can make our way
as best we can
without them.

Rebel.
We can attack the Dominant culture—
try to destroy it,
discredit it,
tear down its heroes,
revise its history
and ours,
paint ours as good
and theirs as evil.
We can try to dominate "Them,"
pass laws to constrain "Them."
We can try to make our way
the dominant way.

Drop out.
We can withdraw from both cultures—
into drugs, alcohol,
insanity.

Crime.
Since the Dominant culture is unfair—
its rules are *their* rules,
its laws, *their* laws,
its opportunities, *their* opportunities—
we can take what we can,
we can steal,
cheat,
lie.
We can break *their* laws,
which isn't crime,
only doing what is fair,
making our way
as best we can
in their culture.

Adopt.
Embrace.
Separate.
Rebel.
Drop Out.
Crime.
All struggling to survive
as the Dominated
among the Dominant.

The Possibility of Transformation

Or we can choose to end the old dance—
first to see it,
then to end it—
to transform the culture

so that it embraces the cultures
of both the Dominant
and the Dominated:
the customs of each,
the speech,
the emotionality,
the history,
the spirituality
of both the Dominant
and the Dominated.

The Dominants will resist—
powerfully.
They will wonder what the fuss is all about.
For them there is no problem,
nothing to solve,
nothing to fix.
Their culture is invisible to them;
it is the water in which they swim,
the air they breathe.
The Dominants are offended
when their culture is made visible,
when it becomes an option
rather than the way things are.
The Dominants will resist,
and if the Dominated persist,
there will be chaos:
A mess,
the disruption of the familiar energy pattern.
And in the chaos,
there is nothing but possibility:
The Dominant crushing the Dominated—

that's possible!

A settling back into the old comfortably uncomfortable
dance—

that's also possible.

A complete rupture of the relationship—

that, too, is possible.

And there is always the possibility of transforming the
culture into some new and unpredictable form.

(Remember when it was unthinkable that women and
Blacks would vote.)

There will be resistance,

but is resistance just resistance?

Or is it also the sound of the old dance shaking?

■

He: Dominant cultures have accomplished great things. You're not
denying that are you?

She: The issue is: Did those great things have to be accomplished over
the bodies of the Dominated? That is the blind reflex. What were
the possibilities of partnership around the life of these systems?
What are the possibilities now?

He: Are you optimistic about *this* transformation?

She: Neither optimistic nor pessimistic—simply painfully aware of the
tragic alternatives. Throughout history, the consequences of this
dance have been devastating.

31 The Terrible Dance of Power

A Terrible Dance

There is a dance that takes place with great regularity,
a terrible dance—
a dance of death and destruction,
human beings killing one another for great and noble causes.
We have danced this dance throughout our history.
We dance it now
in the Balkans,
in Israel,
in Northern Ireland,
in Rwanda,
in the old Soviet Union,
in South Africa,
in Peru,
in Sri Lanka,
in the Philippines,
in El Salvador.

We have danced the dance in years gone by:
in the great American West
with the destruction of the American Indian,
in Turkey
with the destruction of the Armenians,
in Germany
with the destruction of the Jews and Gypsies and homosexuals,
in Cambodia
with the annihilation of millions,
in India
with Hindus and Moslems massacring one another.

Death and destruction
for great and noble causes.

The Dance Begins

There is a nation;
and in that nation,
there are the High-Power people
and the Low-Power people.

The High-Power people control the nation's resources:
Its food, materials, technology, weapons, opportunities.
And there are the Low-Power people.
The High-Power people see themselves as the bearers
of some higher mission:
Manifest Destiny,
The Master Race,
The True Religion,
The Way.

Standing in the way of this mission
are the Low-Power people;
blocking the vision,
defiling it.

The High-Power people see themselves as "We"—
as special,
noble,
righteous,
favored by history
and by God.
And they see the Low-Power people as "Them"—
as insignificant

or dirty
or dangerous
or evil.
Seeing "Them" this way,
the High-Power people can do to "Them"
things they would never do to one another.
They establish rules or laws or customs
that make things better for the "We"
and worse for the "Them."

They may stop the Low-Power people
from practicing their ways;
they may remove them from their territory
or confiscate their property
or enslave them
or exile them
or annihilate them.

They can do all of this
without guilt or shame,
because the Low-Power people are "Them"—
lesser,
insignificant,
dirty,
dangerous,
evil.

Who wouldn't do this to such people?

If the Low-Power people are destroyed,
the dance is ended.
If not,
the dance goes on.

The Low-Power People Respond

The Low-Power people respond—
gently,
fearfully,
rationally,
even apologetically.
(We don't want to make 'Them' angry.")
They cast ballots,
elect representatives,
debate,
demonstrate.

The High-Power People React

To the High-Power people,
the response of the Low-Power people
is out of line—
a complaint,
a threat,
an insult to the dignity of the "We."
("Who are 'They' to complain?")
And the response of the High-Power people is harsh—
requests are ignored,
promises are made
then broken;
they delay;
they ban demonstrations;
they pass new laws;
they intensify the oppression.

Enter the Radicals

A new force develops among the Low-Power people—
a radical force.
The Radicals call for more drastic action—
not accommodation,
but fundamental change;
overthrow the power structure
or separate from the nation.

The Radicals become a "We,"
and all who are not "We"
are "Them."
The High-Power people are "Them,"
but so are the Moderates.
And you can do to "Them"
things you would never do to one another—
you can hurt "Them,"
maim "Them,"
bomb "Them,"
torture "Them,"
annihilate "Them."

The Radicals can do all of this
without guilt or shame
because they see the High-Power people as "Them,"
and they see the Moderates as "Them"—
as lesser,
insignificant,
dirty,
dangerous,
or evil.

Who wouldn't do this to such people?

Enter the Accommodators and the Extremists

In the High-Power group,
there are the Liberals
who want to accommodate the Low-Power people—
redress their grievances,
right their wrongs.

But,
in response to the Radicals' actions,
a new force emerges among the High-Power people—
an Extremist force.
Angered by the Radicals,
threatened by "Them,"
the Extremists stand against *any* accommodation.

The Extremists become a "We,"
and all who are not "We"
are "Them."
The Radicals are "Them";
the supporters of Radicals are "Them";
the Accommodators are "Them."
They are all "Them,"
and you can do to "Them"
things you would never do to one another—
you can hurt "Them,"
maim "Them,"
bomb "Them,"
torture "Them,"
annihilate "Them."

The Extremists can do all of this
without guilt or shame
because they see the Radicals

and the moderates
as "Them"—
as lesser,
insignificant,
dirty,
dangerous,
or evil.

Who wouldn't do this to such people?

Enter the Privileged Radicals

Among the High-Power people,
there emerges a Privileged Radical group—
the privileged sons and daughters of the High-Power people,
who align themselves with the Low-Power Radical group.
The Privileged Radical people
also stand for radical change—
fundamental change in the power structure,
redistribution of wealth, power, and privilege,
or separate homelands
or nations
for the Low-Power people.

The Privileged Radicals see themselves
and the Low-Power Radicals as a "We,"
and all who are not part of the "We"
are "Them."
The High-Power Accommodators are "Them";
the Low-Power Moderates are "Them";
the High-Power Extremists are "Them."
They are all "Them,"
and you can do to "Them"

things you would never do to one another—
you can humiliate "Them,"
hurt "Them,"
maim "Them,"
bomb "Them,"
torture "Them,"
annihilate "Them."

The Privileged Radicals can do all of this
without guilt or shame
because they see the others as "Them"—
as lesser,
insignificant,
dirty,
dangerous,
or evil.

Who wouldn't do this to such people?

Change Partners

Sometimes the Low-Power people win;
they overthrow the High-Power people
and they become the new High-Power people,
seeing themselves as the bearers of a new vision—
a higher vision,
The New Society,
Manifest Destiny,
The New Man,
The Master Race,
The True Religion,
The Way.
And standing in the way of this vision

are the new Low-Power people—
"Them."

And the terrible dance goes on:
"We" humiliate,
"We" hurt,
"We" kill,
"We" maim,
"We" bomb,
"We" hack,
"We" hang,
"We" mine,
"We" strangle,
"We" starve
"Them."
Always justified in what "We" do,
"We" are the right and the righteous.

Who wouldn't do such things to "Them"?

The Dance Goes On

The terrible dance goes on
in Israel,
in the Balkans,
in Rwanda,
in the old Soviet Union,
in South Africa,
in the great cities of America,
in Peru,
in Guatemala,
in Northern Ireland,
in the Philippines.

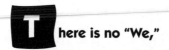

There is no "We,"

There is no "Them,"

There is only You

and Me

and all of Us.

And then the Dance begins.

"Between fanaticism and barbarism there is only one step."
Diderot

"Following a soccer match at least twenty-five Ghanaians were reported hacked, burned and impaled to death."
Boston Globe, _November 12, 1993_

"Imagine asking people who they are and the only thing they can come up with is 'I'm a Croat' or 'I'm a Serb' or whatever. Imagine, these people were born that way and they haven't made any progress since."
Bosnian woman

32 The Sound of the Old Dance Shaking

Systems are not simply collections of individuals,
they are patterns of relationship—
Top/Bottom,
Ends/Middle,
Provider/Customer,
Dominant/Dominated.
We exist only in relationship—
sometimes on one side,
sometimes on the other.
We dance in relationship,
and in the dance,
we grow apart from one another—
becoming the Burdened
and the Oppressed,
the Unsupported
and the Torn,
the Judged
and the Screwed,
the Righteous
and the Wronged.
We dance
without seeing the dance.
On the inside
there is no dance,
only our feelings,
our beliefs—
so solid,
so sure,
"Reality,"
the way things *really* are.

Can we change the dance?
Maybe,

maybe not.
Maybe we will go on dancing
to the end of our days—
not seeing one another,
not loving one another,
misunderstanding,
hurting, and destroying one another.

Or maybe we will see the dance.
And maybe we will stop the dance.
And maybe we will create a new dance.

But first,
there will be the sound of the old dance shaking.

33 Seeing the Dance

He: How can we see the dances when we are in them?

She: We can monitor our own behavior. We can coach one another. We can take a stand for partnership. We can pay attention to our feelings.

Monitoring Our Own Behavior

He: How do we monitor our own behavior?

She: (showing signs of impatience) Just pay attention!

He: Excuse me.

She: The light is on. By now you should be able to see for yourself. Simply pay attention to the relationships you are in, wherever you are—in the classroom, the meeting, the task force. Wherever. Are you Top in a Top/Bottom relationship? Or are you Bottom? Are you an End or a Middle? A Provider or a Customer? Notice where the responsibility is flowing. Pay attention. Is the dance on? And if it is, then you have a choice: Continue the dance or create a new one.

He: I'm not sure I'll always see the dance.

She: You may not, but keep looking. You'll get better at it. In the meantime, you can coach others and ask others to coach you.

He: Coach me?

She: Coach you.

Coaching

We sometimes see the dance in others
when they don't see it in themselves;
just as they see the dance in us
when we are still blind to it.
Each of us has the power
to turn on the lights for the other.

The dance is on.
Don't you see it?
You're pulling that responsibility up to yourself
and away from others.

> *You're taking on all responsibility for the system*
> *and falling into becoming the Burdened Top.*

> *You're taking on all responsibility for resolving*
> *their issues and problems*
> *and falling into becoming the Torn Middle.*

You're taking on all responsibility for delivery
and falling into becoming the Judged Provider.

Do you see that happening?
Do you want to continue the dance
or try a new dance?
Your choice.

Or . . .

You're shifting responsibility
from yourself to others.

>*You're holding "Them" totally responsible for the system*
>*and falling into becoming the whiny, Oppressed Bottom.*

>*You're holding Middle totally responsible for resolving your issues*
>*and falling into becoming the Unsupported End.*

>*You're holding Provider totally responsible for delivery*
>*and falling into becoming the Done-to (Screwed) Customer.*

Do you see that happening?
Do you want to continue that dance
or try a new dance?
Your choice.

Or . . .

You're falling into the Dominant and the Dominated.

Do you see that happening?
Do you want to continue that dance
or try a new dance?
Your choice.

He: This is tough. You call this coaching; some would call it nagging. Criticism. They would resent it.

She: That's the first response . . . the reflex. But we can get past that. If we're committed to partnership, we encourage coaching; we welcome it. We build it into our system. Our stand is to create and sustain partnership.

Taking a Stand for Partnership

We, the members of this system, are fully aware that, in our interactions with one another, we regularly find ourselves in Top/Bottom, Ends/Middle, and Provider/Customer relationships. And we are fully aware of the lure of the Responsibility Dance in which we fall out of the possibility of partnership and into becoming Burdened Tops, Oppressed Bottoms, Unsupported Middles, Judged Providers, and Righteously Done-to Customers.

Our commitment is to avoid the Dance of Blind Reflex and instead create and maintain partnership with one another in whatever process in which we are engaged. We are aware that each of us brings different roles, perspectives, experiences, resources, and skills to the process. Our commitment is to respect and use these differences toward the successful resolution of our joint efforts.

She: And your feelings are often a clue that the dance is on.

Paying Attention to Our Feelings

Our subjective experiences
are not simply personal phenomena;
they are systemic phenomena;
they are clues to our condition within the system.

Burdened? If we are feeling burdened by unmanageable complexity, this may be a clue to us that we are Top in a Top/Bottom relationship and are sucking responsibility up to ourselves and away from others. This awareness opens the possibility of finding ways of sharing the responsibility.

Oppressed? If we are finding much of our energy focused on the Tops—the boss, the president, the politicians, the higher-ups, the parents—if we find ourselves angry at "Them," resentful of "Them," disappointed in "Them," this may be a clue to us that we are Bottom in a Top/Bottom relationship and that we are holding "Them" responsible for our condition and for the condition of the system. This awareness opens the possibility of our examining our own responsibility in those situations in which we are feeling oppressed about.

Unsupported? If we are feeling unsupported by a weak and ineffectual associate, this may be a clue to us that we are an End in an Ends/Middle relationship, and that we are holding the Middle responsible for resolving *our* issues and conflicts. *Could we do easily what we are expecting our Middle to do?* Such awareness opens the possibility of our taking more responsibility for resolving our own issues.

Can't please anyone? If we are feeling weak and ineffective, like we can't please anyone, this may be a clue to us that we are in a Middle position between two or more Ends, and that we are falling into feeling responsible for resolving *their* issues and conflicts. This opens the possibility of our getting more emotional distance for ourselves and finding ways of involving the Ends in resolving their own issues and conflicts.

Unreasonably judged? If we are feeling judged by an unreasonably demanding, disloyal Customer, this may be a clue to us that we have been taking on to ourselves full responsibility for Customer service. Maybe we need to find ways of involving the Customer more in their own delivery process.

Feeling Done-to? If we are feeling righteously done-to by an uncaring, unresponsive Provider, this may be a clue to us that we have abandoned all personal responsibility for obtaining quality service for ourselves. Maybe we need to find ways of becoming more involved in the delivery process—helping the delivery system be more responsive to us.

In this section, we have explored the costs of relational blindness. In system life, we humans are in constantly shifting patterns of relationship with one another. For the most part, this phenomenon of being in relationship is invisible to us. We tend to experience ourselves as whole and autonomous beings rather than as being in relationship. As a consequence, we blindly fall into certain unproductive and destructive dances with one another. We fall out of the possibility of partnership and into relationships of misunderstanding, opposition, antagonism, and destruction.

We also have explored the possibilities of saying "No" to the old dances and creating more satisfying and more constructive new ones. And we have examined strategies for seeing relationship: Being more aware of the dances as we are living them, coaching one another, taking a stand for partnership, and using our feelings as clues to the dance.

For the most part, we human beings do not see the larger system processes of which we are a part. We see individuals within the system, but we do not see "It"—the whole, the system, the family, the team, the business partnership. We do not see "Its" processes as "It" engages with "Its" environment.

In Act Three we will explore the consequences of that blindness. Our focus will be on peer group relationships—on the interactions *among* Tops, *among* Middles, and *among* Bottoms. We will treat each of these groups *as systems* within the larger system of the organization. We shall see how each of these systems blindly and reflexively falls into dysfunctional patterns of interaction: Turf Warfare among the Tops, Alienation among the Middles, GroupThink among the Bottoms.

We also will see how, in our blindness to system processes, we tend to politicize these processes—valuing some and disvaluing others. And we will explore the consequences of such politicization.

Our language is of the organization, but the phenomena we will describe extend far beyond the realm of the organization. For example, we will find striking parallels between the experiences of Top Executive teams and those of parent couples, between Middle Manager peer groups and suburban neighbors, between embattled Worker groups and embattled urban neighborhoods, ethnic groups, and nations. Familiar dances, unproductive and destructive dances, unfolding with great reflexively, without awareness or choice. Dancing in the dark.

Once again, we will explore the possibility of transforming system life from warfare to partnership as we move from blind reflex to enlightened choice.

But not without the sound of the old dances shaking.

34 Are You Sure You Have It All?

He: Are you sure you have it all?

She: I'm sure.

He: But I gave you so much information. It can't all be covered by that one little check mark.

She: It's all covered.

He: Well, what about that inside information about our Top Executives, about all the crazy mixed messages we were getting from the top? And how about that so-called "amicable breakup" at the top over so-called "philosophical differences." That's special, no?

(She looks bored.)

He: Well, what about the Top who took early retirement because of "a long-delayed passion for fly-fishing"?

(No response.)

He: And the "coffee episode"? That tied us up for weeks. Some units had coffee machines in their areas, others didn't. The hearings we held on coffee, . . . committees.

(She chews the eraser but does not write.)

He: And that led to all those other issues about unfairness: different salary and bonus treatment . . . the infighting that broke out among our Middle Managers . . .

(She nods her head but still doesn't lift the pencil.)

He: And the business about the Workers: How they used to be a team, but now half the group doesn't talk to the other half. . . .

She: (stifling a yawn) It's all covered.

He: I don't get it.

She: You will.

He: It's all part of the dance?

She: That's it.

35 Turf Warfare, Alienation, and GroupThink: The DBR Continued

Executive Summary

1. Top group members become territorial and fall into turf battles with one another.

2. Middle group members become alienated from one another; they never become a group.

3. Bottom group members become a cohesive entity, and they fall into pressuring one another into conformity or GroupThink.

4. When relationships among group members break down, the explanations are tied to the personal characteristics of the individuals involved.

Tops Fall into Turf Battles

The Basic Turf pattern:

- Although Tops are collectively responsible for the whole system, they divide responsibility among them.
- Each Top becomes increasingly responsible for his or her own territory and decreasingly responsible for the territory of others and for the whole.
- Tops become more concerned with what is good for their area than for the needs of the system as a whole.
- Instead of being in partnership with one another, Tops feel they need to protect themselves from one another.

Common symptoms of relationship breakdown:

- *Lack of support.* Tops feel unsupported by one another. They feel the need to protect themselves against unwanted incursions into their territory.
- *Status/importance differences.* Some areas of responsibility are considered more important to the operation than others. There are the more important Tops and the less important Tops.
- *Resentment.* Some Tops feel that other Tops are not carrying their fair share of the load.
- *Control battles.* There are struggles over the direction the system as a whole should take: Do we grow quickly or gradually? What is our orientation to our employees (or children)? Are we democratic? Autocratic? Laissez-faire? Do we diversify or stick to our knitting? Do we take financial risks or play it conservatively?
- *Relationship breakdowns.* Relationships that began with promise deteriorate. Partners end up not talking to each other, or the relationship ends in separation, divorce, reorganization. (These promising new reorganizations often end up falling into the same DBR pattern.)

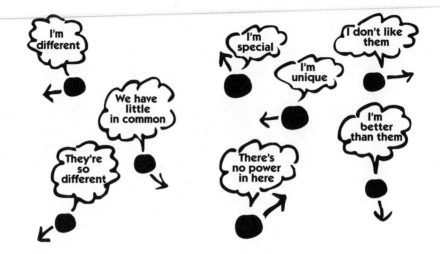

The Basic Alienation pattern:

- Middle groups are non-groups. There is no sense of "We," no common mission or purpose.

- People feel isolated from one another. Even when together (for example, in staff meetings), it is as if their energies are drawn away from one another.

- If you ask members what group they are part of, they are more likely to mention the group they are drawn *toward* (as managers or supervisors or service specialists) rather than the one they are drawn away from (their peers).

Common symptoms of relationship breakdown:

- *Competition.* People are especially sensitive to how they are doing in relationship to others in their group. Am I better than others? Worse than others? Better off? Worse off?

- *Evaluation.* People are quick to make judgments about one another, and these judgments are generally based on *surface* characteristics: How the others dress, how they wear their hair, their physical characteristics, gender, skin color, how they speak, whether they are too emotional or too rational.

- *No power.* People do not feel there is any potential power in this collection.
- *Disinterest.* Given how they feel about one another, it is not surprising that these people have little interest in being together.

Bottom Groups Fall into GroupThink

The Basic GroupThink pattern:

- A "We" mentality develops among the members of the group. Members feel closely identified with one another on the basis of a common cause or purpose or racial, ethnic, or national identity.
- Clear boundaries are drawn between the "We" and all others ("Them").
- Members feel, and exert on one another, a pressure to maintain unity within the group.

Common symptoms of relationship breakdown:

- *Inflated sense of value.* Members have a high (often inflated) sense of their own worth in comparison to "Them."
- *Differential treatment of "Them."* Since the others are seen as lesser than group members, they can be treated in ways one would not use with group members. This differential treatment ranges from

relatively mild (poking fun at one's supervisor) to playing loose with *their* rules, to breaking *their* laws, to defacing or destroying *their* property, to sabotage, to terrorism.

- *Pressure to conform.* There are strong pressures toward *uniformity* within the group. These are pressures that members place on themselves and on one another. Pressures to conform range from subtle to oppressive (coercion, "tough love," reeducation).

- *Exile.* Those who deviate too far and who cannot be brought into line are exiled from the group. As an exile one is subject to the same treatment given "Them" (e.g., scabs and traitors).

- *Splintering.* Apparently irreconcilable factions develop in the group. Factions split off and treat one another as "Thems." An example is the splintering among once uniform religious, political, radical, and philosophical groups.

- *Submergence.* Some members, in order to maintain their place in the group, submerge their differences; they go along with the group story line though they disagree with it. Some members hide their differences from themselves.

- *Village Idiots.* Sometimes diverging members are kept in the group but ignored. They speak, but no one listens. It is as if they are invisible. They are treated by the group as the Village Idiots. Although this is clearly a group dsyfunction, the Village Idiot becomes the "sick" member while the others remain "sane."

How Do Group Members Explain These Relationship Breakdowns?

People believe that their reactions and feelings toward one another are based on real and substantial differences among them. They attribute their relationship breakdowns to the personal characteristics of the parties involved or to an unfortunate mixture of personality types within the group. There is no sense that they have simply fallen into the Dance of Blind Reflex.

He: The more I hear, the more puzzled I get. I don't wake up every morning and say, "Hey gang, I've got a good idea. Why don't we do the Dance of Blind Reflex?" We keep thinking we're unique, making our own choices, dealing with our special situations. And then I see this. Like it's all written out in advance. It's a puzzle.

She: Only from the inside. From the outside, it's all very clear. You will see. I promise you.

He: How does this happen?

She: It happens because we are blind to system processes. Let me give you a summary.

He: Please.

36 Relationship Breakdowns in a Nutshell

She: Top, Middle, and Bottom groups are systems within the system. They are components of a single organization, yet each component struggles to survive in its own unique environment within the organization. Different environments necessitate different survival processes. However, much to our detriment, we get stuck on these survival processes while other important processes are neglected. And the key factor is: We don't see any of this happening. So when relationships break down within our systems, we think it's personal. In a nutshell, it's something like this:

System	Environment	Survival Process	Overlooked Processes	Relationship Breakdown
Top Groups	Complexity and Responsibility	Differentiation	Dedifferentiation Integration	Turf
Middle Groups	Diffusion	Individuation	Integration	Alienation
Bottom Groups	Shared Vulnerability	Integration	Individuation Differentiation	GroupThink

He: I think I need a bit more detail.

**Tops in Complexity:
Stuck on Differentiation**

Put us together in a Top Space—
a space of responsibility
and complexity;
a space in which together
we have responsibility for the system,
the organization,
the family,
the classroom,
the plant,
the team;
a space in which there are
many complex,
difficult,
and changing issues for us to deal with.

We *differentiate*
in order to cope
with that responsibility
and complexity:

"You handle this,
I'll handle that,
she'll handle those,
and he'll handle the other."

Differentiation
is imperative for us;
without it,
we would be overwhelmed,
unable to cope with all of the dangers,
unable to prospect among the opportunities.
However, . . .
we soon become stuck on differentiation.

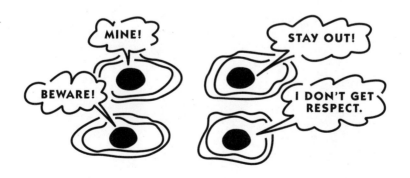

We become complex and specialized.
I elaborate my capacities to perform my functions
and shut off my capacities to perform yours.
You do the same.
We grow increasingly different from one another;
we fall into turf battles—
increasingly territorial,
increasingly responsible for our own differentiations,
decreasingly responsible for the system as a whole.
We fall into relationship problems—
not feeling respected for our contributions,
not feeling supported,
not trusting or feeling trusted,
battling over the direction
the system as a whole should take.
And when we don't see systems,
all of these feelings seem like reality to us,
the way things *really* are.
It's you and me
and the peculiarities of our situation.

It's funny how this turned out, isn't it?
When we began,
we thought we were the perfect
executive team,
couple,
business partners.

38 The Success of a Business, the Failure of Its Partners

Until recently Charles and Edgar were partners (Tops) in a department store business. What began twenty-five years ago with a single, understocked store struggling to survive in a quiet neighborhood gradually grew into a chain of five busy and successful department stores, well situated in an active, urban, shopping area.

As the business grew and the partners prospered, their personal relationship deteriorated. What had begun in friendship and a shared determination to succeed, evolved into a painful history of continuous and escalating conflict. And then the partnership ended.

The pattern of conflict—toward the end at least—was clear and consistent. Each player had the other neatly pegged: Edgar was the reckless *expansionist,* and Charles was the overly cautious *conservative.*

Generally, Edgar wanted to move more quickly on business matters than did Charles: Expand, develop new departments, open new stores, adopt new management control systems, hire and fire personnel, switch from one buying service to another, invest large sums of money in "good buys," and so forth.

Charles, by contrast, was consistently on the side of caution: Maintaining the status quo or pressing for slower and more secure development, fiscally conservative, and more patient with store managers, personnel, and vendors.

■

From a systems perspective, one might describe this as a healthy process. Isn't it beautiful to see how the system is differentiating, how it is exploring its possibilities? What kind of system shall we be? How shall we grow? One might even speculate that the tension between these two emerging differentiations is a healthy process—a creative tension that keeps the system from either expanding beyond its capacity to survive or sinking into zero-growth death. One might reasonably speculate that that creative tension is what accounted for the system's steady growth.

Neither Charles nor Edgar was seeing the system. To them, this was purely a struggle between personalities. And so the relationship became personalized rather than systemized; and as such, it fell into the familiar pattern of differentiation leading to "stuck on differentiation," leading to Turf Warfare, leading to polarization, leading to the dissolution of the partnership.

For Edgar, Charles was the stumbling block, the naysayer standing in the way of business progress. And for Edgar, the naysaying went beyond business; he felt that Charles neither liked nor respected him. He felt that he was too often dismissed, that he was working daily beside a man who doubted his intelligence, failed to respect his judgment, disliked him personally, and refused to give his ideas the full hearing they deserved. As a result, Edgar's attacks on Charles carried more than a rational analysis of the pros and cons of particular decisions; they bore the added emotionality of one who feels unloved, unrespected, and unheard.

Charles, on the other hand, felt that for years he had been living on the edge of disaster. He saw Edgar as a reckless gambler who needed to be controlled if the business was to survive. Charles feared that an unbridled Edgar would keep the business and the partnership in a perpetual state of chaos and would stretch the financial capacity of the business to the breaking point. And beyond business matters, Charles often felt menaced by Edgar's personal style. He saw Edgar as irrational and abusive. He couldn't discuss anything calmly with him. If Charles raised an objection, Edgar would shout and scream and abruptly end the conversation.

After years of turmoil marked by periodic threats of separation, Edgar bought out Charles' share of the business, and the partnership came to an end.

■

She: Differentiation is such a beautiful process. It's proof that the system is *alive*, that it is elaborating its possibilities. Of course, not all differentiations turn out to be functional. Some become blind alleys. But what's to be appreciated is the fact that they all reflect the system's attempt to survive and develop.

He: Are you saying that this whole breakdown between Charles and Edgar was systemic? They did seem to have some powerful personality differences.

She: Of course they did, but it is the systemic craziness that did them in. Systemic craziness multiplies interpersonal craziness.

He: They seemed such stereotypes: Edgar *always* reckless, Charles *always* cautious.

She: When we get stuck on differentiation, we polarize. We *make* one another into stereotypes.

He: That's a neat trick. How do we do it?

She: Let's assume that Charles and Edgar don't start out as stereotypes. Charles is more conservative than Edgar, but he also has an expansive side. And Edgar is more expansive than Charles, but he also has his conservative side. So now let's say an issue comes up, and there's a choice to be either conservative or expansive. What do you think Charles and Edgar will do?

He: They'll probably go with their strong side: Edgar will go expansive, and Charles will go conservative.

She: Right. And that's all they ever see of one another. They never see the other side.

He: So Edgar starts to feel that if he doesn't push for expansion, no one ever will.

She: Exactly. And that makes him very nervous, so he feels he must push harder.

He: And the same thing happens with Charles. He never sees any signs of caution from Edgar, which makes him very nervous, so he pushes harder to conserve.

She: And now we have a perfectly antagonistic set of stereotypes.

He: Beautiful on the outside, deadly on the inside.

Learning from Experience: A Good Second Marriage

A colleague told me about a remarkable group of Tops. "These people are like survivors of bad first marriages," he said. "What's special about them is that they learned from their mistakes and are committed to not repeating them." Each of these Tops, in previous positions, had had painful experiences with the personal and organizational consequences of Turf Warfare. And each was committed to creating something more constructive in this new organization. Their motto: Never again!

How do they do it?

They spend considerable time "walking in one another's shoes." They all have their own areas of responsibility, yet they arrange to spend considerable time together: Regularly traveling together, sharing information, learning about one another's arenas.

They have become good coaches to one another. Each of them knows full well what it is to be a Burdened Top, and they are experts at spotting one another's dysfunctional responses to overload. "When we see one of us racing off the cliff, someone's there to slow them down."

They have invested a good deal of authority in their Middles, which has opened up considerable space for the Tops to deal with issues that would otherwise have been neglected or treated in less depth.

They open their territories to one another. It is not unusual for them to come together to focus their energies on what was generally considered someone's functional responsibility. For example, when it was time to rethink the organization wide incentive plan, it became a collaborative project for the Top team, rather than "Human Resources' business."

My colleague says: "It works. They are a team. Ideas germinate in that group and blossom out. They look forward to working with one another."

■

He: So maybe that's what it takes—one bad experience to learn from.

She: Unfortunately, not everyone learns from experience. If you're committed to believing that the last bad experience was due to an unfortunate mix of personalities . . .

He: . . . or to "philosophical differences" . . .

She: . . . then there's nothing learned, and you're ready to start the same cycle over again.

40 Help! No Recovering Top Groups Sighted

I have been searching my memory for examples of Recovering Top Groups, that is, Top Groups that, having fallen into Turf Warfare, have been able to recover and find their way back into partnership. No luck. What keeps coming back to me are example after example of permanent failures in Top systems: Turf Warfare, breakdown, dissolution of the system. Once it's broken, it stays broken. (Even as I write this, the morning newspaper tells of one more partnership that began with promise and ended in breakdown. This time it was two restauranteurs; the reason, the ever-popular "philosophical differences.")

My own life has been touched again and again by disastrous Top group experiences: My father and uncle became business partners and ended their lives not speaking to one another. The same fate befell my two brothers. I went into business with my dearest friend, and not only did the business dissolve, but so did our friendship. Add to this the collapse of my first marriage, and you have quite a record of failure in the Top system. This qualifies me (an understatement) as an expert on the pitfalls of the Top system. I do believe, however, that this difficulty in identifying break through from Turf Warfare is more than a personal or familial matter.

Whenever a systemic breakdown occurs—whether in Top, Middle, or Bottom systems—the breakdown is always experienced as personal. The fault lies with you or with me or with our particular mix of characteristics. And the explanations feel solid—the way things *really* are. And if you were to suggest that these breakdowns are not personal but systemic, you should expect resistance—not relief. That is true of all three systems, but there is an added element in the Top system that contributes an emotional bite to the breakdown. For the most part, we do not choose our membership in Middle and Bottom systems; we find ourselves there. This is not the case with Top systems; we *choose* our membership in these. We choose our marriage and business partners: Top Executive teams are assembled on the basis of exceptional mixtures of talents; friends and relatives feel that their history and love for one another will ensure business success. And it is under these conditions of choice that failure is particularly painful. We begin with such promise; but the more powerful the promise, the greater the sense of loss, disappointment, and betrayal. It's one thing to treat strangers this way, but to treat friends and relations this way is unforgivable. The separations become irreconcilable. It would take a terrible shaking of the dance to effect a transformation.

So I am still waiting for that first recovery in the Top system. I'm waiting for Edgar to suddenly see the light and slap himself on the forehead. "My God!" he'll say. "I see it now. There's nothing wrong with Charles . . . or with me. What we have here is a failure in differentiation. Charles and I are OK. The problem is not with us, and the solution is not to *fix* us. The solution is to see how, together, we can master this space of complexity and responsibility."

I'm still waiting.

■

He: Short of waiting, isn't there something more productive we can do?
She: We can warn people. *Warning: You are entering the Top system!*

41 Advice for the Top Team

This is a warning to all Top Teams:

Newly married couples,
Newly formed executive teams,
New business partners.

Caution: You are entering the Top Space—
a space of *complexity*
and *responsibility.*

Your life is about to change.

Personally, your mood is likely to shift
from light to heavy—
from feeling responsible for yourself
to feeling responsible for others
(sometimes very many others),
from feeling relatively carefree
to chronic worrying.

Your relationships with your partner(s)
are subject to strain.
You may be entering this partnership
convinced that you are the perfect team.
Those feelings are subject to dramatic change.

Do not believe that you are immune to these processes.
You and your partner(s) may be very special people,
but these processes are not about people,
they are about living in the Top Space.
Strange things can happen to the nicest people
when they get together in the Top Space.

Pursue the following steps, and not only will you save your relationship from deteriorating, you will deepen and strengthen it well beyond its current condition.

Your challenge in the Top Space is to become adept at managing complexity and responsibility without becoming overwhelmed. The general strategies are:

Keep it simple.
Differentiate with zest.
Dedifferentiate with zest.

147

1. *Keep it simple.* Watch out for the tendency to take on responsibility for everything. The Top Space is complex enough without your assuming responsibility for things others could be handling. A major aspect of your Top responsibility is the ability to create responsibility in others.

2. *Differentiate with zest.* This is not likely to be a problem. It will happen. Circumstances will force differentiation on you. Your situation is complex; in order to cope with that complexity and not be overwhelmed by it, you will find yourselves differentiating—certain partners taking on primary responsibility for certain functions, others taking on primary responsibility for other functions.

   Pursue your differentiations with zest; become expert in them and perform them diligently and elegantly.

3. *Dedifferentiate with zest.* This is what will make or break your partnership. Dedifferentiation does not come naturally in the Top Space. You need to work at it. Here your goal is to maintain and strengthen your *commonality.*

   - *Vision.* Come to agreement on a common vision for this system (family, organization, partnership). What are your fondest wishes for what it will become? This will become an important foundation to revisit when there is tension among the partners.
   - *Shared information.* Regularly share information with one another regarding the events, issues, difficulties, and choices in your respective areas of responsibility.
   - *Mutual coaching.* Create coaching relationships with one another such that each of you, as coach to the other(s), becomes fully committed to the other's success as well as to your own. Mutual coaching is likely to be *the* most powerful process for maintaining and strengthening both your partnership and the system for which you have joint responsibility.
   - *Interchangeability.* Create regular opportunities to walk in the others' shoes, experiencing their worlds and the issues they are dealing with.
   - *Joint task forces.* Find opportunities to partner with one another when new issues arise that fall outside your areas of responsibility.

He: Dedifferentiation! That's six syllables!

She: Seven. But keep your eye on dedifferentiation. It is a critical process for system success. And it is the one most frequently overlooked.

Wherever there is differentiation—

the elaboration of our differences—

special attention needs to be given to

dedifferentiation:

developing and maintaining our commonality.

Top systems exist in environments of

complexity and responsibility;

in order to survive in those environments,

Top systems differentiate.

Then they get stuck on differentiation,

and that's when Turf Warfare sets in.

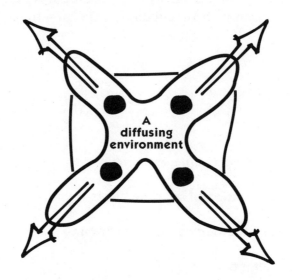

Put us together
in a *diffusing* space—
a space that draws us *away* from one another,
out toward other compelling
individuals,
groups,
activities—
and we become a collection of independent "I"s.

Even when together
in our groups or neighborhoods,
we feel separate,
unique—
having little in common with one another,
feeling competitive with one another,

being evaluative of one another.
It is crystal clear to us:
This is no group,
and there is no power in here.

Feeling as we do about one another,
we stay apart
("Why would I spend more time with such people?")
which reinforces our alienation
and completes the cycle.

And when we don't see systems,
all of these perceptions, evaluations, and feelings
are reality to us—
the way things *really* are.
Alienation is the illusion of the Middle Space.

43 Alienation Among the Middles

When we don't see systems,
we are at their mercy.

Of the three classes in the Power Lab, the Middles are invariably the most disintegrated. The Middles share a common house and a common title (Middles or Managers), they eat at a common table, they sometimes meet together, but they remain a collection of autonomous individuals. The Middle class rarely has a position or platform of its own in the society; it functions between the conflicting positions and platforms of the Elite and the Immigrants. Individual Middles are drawn to aligning themselves with either the Elite or the Immigrants or to remaining torn between the two. The Middle house is usually an uninviting place; it is clear that nothing of much significance happens there.

In the Middle Space, even when we are together, it is as if our backs are turned to one another.

Consider the following:

The Middles are having dinner "together," that is, they are sharing the same table.

Stan has been trying to get the attention of his associate Middles, but he is having little success. "I need to talk with you," he says. There is no response. Each of Stan's associates is busily at work on his or her own business.

Court Officer Carla is shuffling through a stack of proposals she has received from the Immigrants. She is under pressure from her boss to get these proposals sorted out. Carla is also disconcerted by the fact that her rent is due and she hasn't yet been paid.

"They're giving me a hard time," says Stan, referring to the Immigrants. Still no response.

Kerry is working diligently on a financial report for her boss. She is responsible for the store and supplies, and her boss has been complaining about the poor quality of her reporting. She hardly glances up as Stan speaks.

Bill, who is responsible for employment, is preparing a work status report. His boss just came by the table complaining that the report was past due and asking that it be ready in thirty minutes.

"The Immigrants are giving me a hard time," says Stan, still standing by the table. That catches Court Officer Carla's attention. "Are there any infractions?" she asks. As Court Officer, infractions are Carla's business. She shows little interest in whatever other problems Stan might be having. "I'll assume everything's legal unless you tell me otherwise," she says as she returns to perusing her stack of proposals.

Stan stands awkwardly at the table. Finally, he speaks (to no one in particular). "Should I just start talking?"

Might as well, Stan.

■

He: I've had many such "conversations" with my Middle peers.

She: You are not alone. Fear and loathing in the Middle Space is not exactly an uncommon condition—members feeling unique, having little in common, feeling competitive and evaluative, believing that there's no power in this Middle group, there's no point in being together.

He: As you run down that list, I find myself thinking as much about my neighbors as about my organizational peers. We're also competitive, evaluative, unique. We're focused on who does what with their lawn or pool or deck. You know what I mean: One trying to outdo the other. Folks not getting along with one another.

She: Much of our lives is spent in this diffusing space. We are pulled apart from one another and fall into the illusion of alienation.

Exercise

Take yourself to a train or bus station—
the perfect diffusing space.
Most of the folks you see don't belong here;
they are heading somewhere else.
Find a bench where you can sit and watch all the people
passing by.
And watch yourself watching them:
This one is attractive, and this one is not;
this one does funny things with his hair, and this one
dresses strangely;
this one is too emotional, and that one talks too loudly.
An unending stream of evaluations.

He: I don't have to go to the train station to have that experience. Just about any weekly staff meeting will do. What a bunch of alienated misfits we are.

She: Yes, but are you prepared to give that up?

He: I don't understand.

She: Are you prepared to face the possibility that that collection of misfits could become a powerful system; that you could come to like and respect one another; that you could become a powerful and effective force in your organization; that you could become a useful support system for one another; that your Tops would really value you as a team; that your Workers would see all of you as providing effective and coordinated leadership? Are you prepared to face that possibility?

He: You've got to be kidding.

She: Are you prepared to face the fact that I'm not kidding?

44 Can Alienated Middles Become a Powerful System?

He: Is there anything Middles can do so that they're *not* alienated?

She: Yes, but first you have to learn to distrust your experience.

He: *Distrust my experience?*

She: Aha! I hear the sound of the old dance shaking. When you are in the Middle Space, it all seems so real to you. It really *is* clear that you have little in common with the others, that there's no power in here, that you're not comfortable with one another, and so forth. This is the evidence of your senses. So why would you even consider becoming an integrated "We" with this collection of misfits?

So the very first step is to recognize that these very solid feelings and evaluations you have may not be the *cause* of your alienation from one another. More likely, they are the *result* of that alienation.

He: Come again.

She: You think that the reason you don't integrate with one another is because of how you feel about one another. ("Why would I want to integrate with *these* people?") In fact, it's just the other way around. You feel the way you do about one another *because* you don't integrate. *And if you did integrate, you would feel very differently about one another.*

If this appears to be too big a pill to swallow, consider the following: We have conducted many hundreds of organization exercises over the past twenty-five years. In each exercise, people are randomly assigned to Top, Middle, or Bottom groups. At some point we ask people to describe their relationships with their group members. The comparison of the Middle and Bottom group experiences is particularly striking. With great regularity, Bottoms speak very positively about their groups, using such terms as *teamwork, sharing, supportive, high energy.* As a group, Bottoms say, "We could do the job if only *they* . . ." With equal regularity, Middles describe themselves as a non-group. It is particularly interesting to hear Middles describe their groups very positively, only to find out that the groups they are referring to are their *Worker* groups—since the notion of Middles as a group is too ludicrous to even consider. With Middles, it is only a question of the degree of alienation between them—from simply having nothing to do with one another to extreme competitiveness and interpersonal tension.

So explanations of Middle alienation in terms of companies' hiring practices, social Darwinism, or genetic disposition simply won't do. It is clear that had those Middles been put together in Bottom groups, there is every likelihood they would have described themselves in terms of teamwork, sharing, support, "We," and so forth. This is precisely what this systemic lens is all about.

"Middle group" is generally an oxymoron:
If they're Middles, they're not a group;
and if they're a group, they're not Middles.

Generally, that's the case.
Generally,. . . . but not always.

It is the exception that points the way to possibility.

Some years ago, I was delivering a lecture on Middle power and powerlessness. The lecture was, for the most part, pure theory: *Here is the nature of Middle Space. Here is what happens to a collection of sane, healthy, competent people when you put them together in that space. Here is how they disintegrate personally and collectively. And here is what you must do if you want to create powerful teams of Middles.*

The theory was solid; it was backed by years of observations of Middle groups in our organizational and community simulations. And although I was not at the time much involved in "real world" organizations, I began to hear from folks who were that these were precisely the dynamics they were living with.

The First Mutation

One story I told had to do with the first Middle group mutation I had experienced. It came during a multiple-day workshop. Each day there was an organization exercise involving Tops, Middles, Bottoms, and Customers. On the first day, the traditional Middle group dance unfolded: The disintegration of Middles individually and collectively. On the second day, a new group of Middles approached the exercise determined to show everyone what *real* Middles could do. The results were the same: Personal and collective disintegration. It was on the third day that the mutation appeared.

The Simple Agreement

The members of this third group of Middles made a simple agreement with one another: They were to meet at the beginning and middle of each workperiod—just Middles, no Tops—to share information, identify issues they all needed to work on, and stay coordinated. The agreement was to meet *no matter what competing pressures there were*. For it had been made clear that in this diffusing Middle Space, there were always competing pressures: Your work group needs to see you *now* or the Tops need to meet with you or the Customers need you. The Middles would make it clear to others that these Middle meetings were commitments and were critical to organizational health and customer service.

As is the case with all transformations, there was resistance. No one appreciated being put off. *Why do Middles have to meet?* The Middles persisted, and the transformation was total. In the end, Tops and Bottoms agreed that the Middles played the central role in the organization's success. Both saw the Middles as a strong and effective unit. The Middles seemed to be in synch with one another; they did not experience disintegration personally or collectively. They felt like a team. (A remarkable outcome for Middles!) They had alleviated the burdens of Tops, provided strong, informed, and consistent leadership for their Workers, and developed solid relationships with one another. And all of this by simply making *and sticking to* the commitment to meet regularly with one another.

The First Practical Application

Bob DuBrul, a consultant, was in the audience that day. Bob and I were not to meet face to face for several years, but when we did, he told me the following story. The lecture had set him thinking: This familiar disintegrated Middle group pattern seemed to fit many of his client systems. Were powerful Middle teams possible? Could this commitment to regular integration work? Bob was hesitant. He knew there would be considerable resistance from the Middles themselves. The usual litany: *Why should we get together? We have little in common. We don't get along with one another. There's no power in here.* So Bob held off.

That summer, his daughter, Tresa Amrani, became director of counselors at a summer camp. In one of their conversations, she let on how burdened she was by the complexities and responsibilities of the job. There were issues she needed to deal with from her counselors, from the camp directors, from activities directors, from parents, and more. She was unable to keep up. She was particularly troubled by the decisions her counselors were bringing to her, matters she felt they themselves were perfectly capable of handling. There were other issues among the counselors: Competition, personal squabbles, lack of coordination, inconsistency.

Tresa's situation brought back to Bob the picture of Middle group disintegration and the possibilities of Middle power. They discussed the situation, and Tresa launched the first (to my knowledge) "real world" application of the theory. She created the counselors as a self-regulating Middle team. Their charge was to work collectively to manage the bulk of the day-to-day operations of the camp. They met regularly—without Tresa—to do whatever business had to be done.

The Sound of Two Dances Shaking

There were resistances as one would predict. There were two dances being disrupted here: The Top/Bottom dance between Tresa and the counselors and the Alienated Middle dance going on among the counselors. There were numerous issues that needed to be dealt with (some of which we'll discuss below), but the experiment was a resounding success. The counselors basically ran the operation, and Tresa was freed up to do her Top business.

Tresa's experience gave Bob the confidence to begin to work with Middle integration in his own practice. It was some years later that Bob and I met and Bob told me this story and about his other rich experiences in working with Middle integration.

When the shift works (and it doesn't always work), the transformation of the Middle Space is nearly miraculous. Bob describes one plant at which the Plant Manager claims his integrating Middle team now runs the bulk of the day-to-day operations of the plant. This Plant Manager's boss says that, of all the Plant Managers, this one is the only one having fun. Much of the Plant Manager's burden is relieved by the integrating Middle team. Workers have great respect for these Middles: They see them as coordinated and as providing strong, consistent, and informed leadership. The compensation structure has been modified to fit the new reality, such that the Middles are paid 50 percent for how well they individually manage their units and 50 percent for how well they collectively integrate the whole.[5]

"We Need Your Leadership"

There is one other piece to this story. One day Bob was called in by the Top of an integrating Middle group. One of the Middles had come to the Top saying that the Middles were stuck on a particular issue. "We need your leadership," said the Middle. (What Top can resist that call?) The Top asked Bob what he thought he should do. Bob said he'd think about it. Bob called Tresa.

"Exactly the same thing happened to me," she said. "One of the counselors said they couldn't work out some issue and they needed me."

"What did you do?"

"I told them they could work it out."

"And did they?"

"They did."

So Bob went back to the Top and advised him to stay out of the issue and encourage the Middles to resolve it themselves, which they did. And the lesson for Bob and for all of us is: It is precisely in having to face and deal with the most difficult issues that the possibility of Middle power lies.

"It" Never Works

Some experiments with Middle integration have worked, some haven't. One Middle once said to me, "We tried integration, and it didn't work. Nothing happened." Well, it's true: Nothing ever happens. I imagined these Middles sitting silently in a room, tapping their feet, glancing at their watches, waiting for some miracle to strike. It doesn't happen that way. For Middle integration to work, two comfortably uncomfortable dances need to be disrupted: The Top/Bottom dance and the Alienated Middles dance. There are myriad opportunities for resistance. Are Middles ready to give up their Bottomness and become Top? Is Top ready to allow Middles to be Top? Are Middles (all of them) ready to give up their alienation from one another? There are many people and many opportunities to say "No." And "No" can end the process.

As usual it comes down to how one treats "No." Is "No" the end of the process? Or is it the sound of two dances shaking?

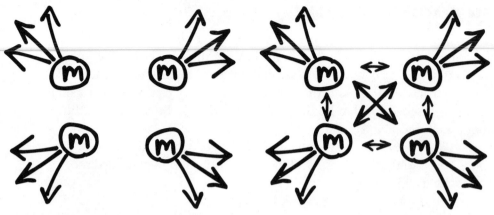

When Middles Are Dis-Integrated	**When Middles Integrate**
1. They are alone, unsupported, not part of Top or Bottom, not even connected with one another.	They have a supportive peer group.
2. They are uninformed, surpriseable.	Through regular sharing of information, they are highly informed.
3. They are focused on their group's needs.	They are focused on what their groups need *and* on what the system needs.
4. They are seen by Workers as weak, uninformed, fractionated.	They are seen as "having the goods," being consistent, and providing strong leadership.
5. Uneven practices among Middles are seen as inconsistent, unfair.	They are seen as fair, consistent, coordinated.
6. Top is responsible for system integration.	Middles handle system integration. Top is freed up to do Top business.
7. Top complaints: Middles aren't entrepreneurial enough.	Middles identify and work on needed initiatives.
Can't get initiatives down through the Middles.	Top puts initiatives into the Middle group; they work them around and then move them into the system consistently and quickly.
Don't get consistent information from Middles.	Do get consistent information from Middles.

46 How to Create Powerful Middle Teams

*In Middle groups,
special attention needs to be paid to integration.
In the diffusing environment,
integration will not happen naturally;
it has to be worked at
rigorously.*

1. Believe that it's possible.

2. Create a compelling *mission* for yourselves. What are your fondest wishes about what this group can be? *Externally*—what can it accomplish in the world? *Internally*—what kinds of relationships do you want to create with one another?

3. Get past the myths of alienation. Find out who you are and what really matters to you. Learn about one another's *personal* interests, projects, passions, or missions.

4. Support one another in pursuing your personal projects.

5. Support one another in pursuing the group's mission.

6. Create regular mechanisms for sharing information, supporting one another, coaching one another.

7. Treat these mechanisms as sacred commitments.

8. Be ready to be surprised.

9. Remember: Alienation is an illusion of the Middle Space.

■

He: That's a great idea.

She: But?

He: But it wouldn't work with my group.

She: Why?

He: Why? Because we're unique, we have little in common, we don't get along with one another, we're competitive, there's no point in our getting together, there's no power in here . . .

I'm kidding. I'm kidding.

She: I hope so.

Top systems exist in environments of

complexity and responsibility;

in order to survive in those environments,

Top systems differentiate.

Then they get stuck on differentiation,

and that's when Turf Warfare sets in.

Middle systems exist in

diffusing environments;

in order to survive in those environments,

Middle systems individuate.

Then they get stuck on individuation,

and that's when Alienation sets in.

47 Bottom Systems in Vulnerability: Stuck on Integration

From "I" to "We"

Put us together
in a space of *vulnerability*,
a space in which some important aspect of our existence
feels threatened—
our livelihood,
our neighborhood,
our way of life,
our nation,
our religion or ethnic group—
and we a become a "We,"
integrated components of some larger "It"—
the Group,
the Neighborhood,
the Nation
the Religion
the Race.

The "We" is greater than the "I"

We become one with that entity,
enhanced in it—
stronger,
timeless,
nobler,
heroic.
There is something special about
our Neighborhood,
we Workers,
our Nation,
our Religion,
our Social Class,
even *our* Sports Team.

"We" against "Them"

There is no "We" without some "Them"—
Management,
another Neighborhood,
another Nation,
another Ethnic Group,
another Religion.
The enhancement of the "We"
allows us to do damage to others.
When we are stuck in the "We,"
we can abuse these others,
hurt them,
oppress them,
and even destroy them
with little shame or guilt,

because in our "We"-ness
it is crystal clear that the "Them"
is different,
lesser,
than the "We."

Trouble Within the "We"

When we are stuck in "We,"
there is no room for the One Who Disagrees.
When we are stuck in "We,"
the One Who Disagrees becomes dangerous
to others
and to oneself.

When the Ones Who Disagree slip too far from the "We,"
the "We" grow anxious—
We must bring the Ones Who Disagree back into line—
love them,
educate them,
coerce them into line.
And if we can't bring them into line,
we must shun them,
confine them,
jail them,
exile them,
or eliminate them.

And when the Ones Who Disagree slip too far from
the "We,"
the "Ones" grow anxious too.
The "Ones" need the "We,"

so the "Ones" hide their disagreement from the "We";
they go along with the "We"
even though they disagree;
they go along
with false zest
or in apathy
and shame.

And sometimes
the Ones Who Disagree hide their disagreement even
from themselves
and become mysteriously ill.

48 Immigrant Martha Has a Breakdown

The following case comes from an early Power Lab. It is one of many that helped us see into life within the "We."

A negotiating session is in progress. Involved are representatives of the Elite, the Managers (Middles), and the Immigrants. The society has been fractionated for days, and it has been a struggle to bring all parties to the table. But here they are at last. A specific set of agenda items has been agreed to. Members of the society not directly involved in the negotiations are invited to observe the process but are prohibited from interfering with it.

Immigrant Martha is standing behind the negotiating table observing. The complete agenda has been laid out, and work on the first few items is proceeding. The process is rational and orderly: Items are presented and clarified, offers are made, caucuses are held, counter-proposals are offered. All in all, a very different climate exists from that which characterized previous interchanges among Elite, Managers, and Immigrants.

Martha becomes distraught. Fighting back tears, she runs from the room. The Negotiators pause momentarily, then continue their work. A few minutes later, Martha returns. It is obvious that she has been crying, and she is trembling now. She interrupts the negotiating process, sobbing while fighting to get the words out: "We (Immigrants) are in a degraded position. . . . We are asking for minimal things. . . . " She sobs, catches her breath, and musters the strength to continue. Then, her body trembling, her face flushed in rage, she shouts: "I . . . AM . . . SICK . . . AND . . . TIRED . . . OF . . . IT. THAT IS WHERE *I* AM. . . . I CANNOT TAKE THIS ANYMORE. . . . I CANNOT WATCH THIS ANYMORE. . . . IT IS TOO DEGRADING. . . . I AM LEAVING." She storms out of the room, and the negotiating process stops.

Gerri, an Immigrant Negotiator, says, "This is beyond our capacity to handle. It is beyond the scope of the game. Martha is an unstable person. She's fragile and she's going to need competent psychological help." Other Immigrants nod their heads in agreement. Martha has been shaky of late: Withdrawn, crying, displaying bursts of anger not only at the Elite and Managers but, more commonly, at her associate Workers. "She's an unstable person," says Gerri, "and she needs professional help."

■

When we don't see systems, we see individual personalities. Our explanations are personal, and our solutions are personal. Fix the individual. In this case, fix Martha. When we see systems, quite another world opens up to us. What we have here is not a personal problem but a social disease—a disorder of the "We." What we have here is a failure in differentiation.

Within the "We," two competing forces come into play. There are powerful pressures to remain a uniform "We," for in this solidarity lies strength. However, working against that uniformity are the variations that *inevitably* develop within the "We."

Given enough time, *in all bottom groups,* a directional differentiation develops regarding the best way to handle our vulnerability to "Them"—should we be tough or soft with "Them"? Should we be polite or confrontative? Should we enter into negotiations or take direct action? The form and intensity of the differences vary from system to system. (In one setting, "tough" might mean "Let's complain," and "soft" might mean "Let's not"; much further along the continuum, "soft" might mean "Let's not kill women and children.") Whatever the form and intensity, the directional differentiation occurs with great predictability, whether in Worker groups in the organization, in oppressed groups in society, or in revolutionary groups.

In its vulnerability, the system—unable to tolerate the internal pressure caused by differentiation—resolves this tension in any number of ways, each of which serves to maintain the integrity of the "We":

- By fractionating into separate (and usually mutually antagonistic) "We's"
- By coercing dissenters into line
- By exiling dissenters
- By jailing dissenters
- By executing dissenters
- By declaring dissenters insane

One of the more interesting resolutions—and one that has bearing on Martha's case—is the emergence of the Village Idiot. Sometimes the system maintains its integrity by submerging a conflicting differentiation. *Dissenters become invisible:* Their suggestions are ignored; they are treated as eccentrics; they speak but no one listens. They are "crazy" while the rest of the village remains "sane."

A Systemic Cure

Martha did not get her personal fix. She remained apathetic, listless, and depressed throughout the remainder of the society's life. However, she did get her cure, which turned out to have ramifications beyond Martha.

In my role as societal Anthropologist, I happened to compile a list of "Key Immigrant Decisions." Throughout the life of the society, issues arose requiring decisions by the Immigrants: Do we go this way or that? The choices were always on the order of: Do we take a hard or soft line with "Them"? Do we go along or resist, cooperate or fight?

Being a highly integrated system, no individual decisions were made. The Immigrants would caucus, discuss the issue, and come up with the *group* decision.

Their issues included:

- Do we accept their wage hike proposal?
- Do we participate in their community improvement process?
- Should Gerri leave the group and accept a promotion into Middle Management?
- Do we show up for court?
- Do we agree to participate in the negotiation process?

Now the community experience was over, and we were debriefing it. We had reviewed the Elite experience and the Manager experience, and now the Immigrants were at the front of the room—seven happy people and one depressed Martha. We spent some time talking about various aspects of the Immigrant experience. Martha was uncommunicative throughout.

Then I brought out my list of key decisions. We reviewed the decisions sequentially. I asked people to recall, as best they could, what their *individual* positions had been on each decision. I asked them to estimate the intensity of their feelings by using a ten-point rating system: If they felt strongly in a given direction, they would score themselves 10/0; if they mildly favored one direction over the other, they might score themselves 6/4, and so forth.

We proceeded decision by decision, reviewing each issue, having people make their judgments privately, and then having them enter their judgments on a newsprint chart. This was a laborious process, and I was not at all confident that it would lead anywhere.

The data for the first decision are presented in Table 48.1. Martha and Tim were 10/0 for resistance, and all other group members were also for resistance, but with lesser intensity. The data for subsequent decisions repeated this pattern.

Table 48.1   Decision 1

	MARTHA	TIM	ROGER	GERRI	BOB	NANCY	HANK	ANDY
RESIST	10	10	6	6	8	8	7	7
COOPERATE	0	0	4	4	2	2	3	3

Then on Decision 7 (Should we enter into negotiations with the Elite?), the pattern shifted dramatically:

Table 48.2   Decision 7

	MARTHA	TIM	ROGER	GERRI	BOB	NANCY	HANK	ANDY
RESIST	10	5	4	2	5	4	4	2
COOPERATE	0	5	6	8	5	6	6	8

At this point, we talked about the data. Immigrants were struck by their early pattern of resistance: Although they were in agreement, there were large differences in the intensity of feeling among them. They were also struck by the solidarity of Martha's and Tim's 10/0 responses, which brought back memories of Martha's early enthusiasm, involvement, and leadership in the group.

Then we talked about Decision 7, and Martha became quite engaged at this point. *It became clear that Martha's resistance was always of a different order than that of her associate Immigrants.* For her, the goal was radical systems change: The creation of an egalitarian society in which there were no Elite, Managers, and Immigrants—only citizens—with no distinctions in housing, work, pay, and so forth. For other Immigrants, the issue had more to do with involvement in decisions affecting their lives. They were perfectly willing to accept the three-class societal structure so long as their participation in decision making was assured. So when the decision was made to enter into direct negotiations with the Elite on specific issues of labor, housing, pricing, and so on *while accepting the basic societal structure,* the split between Martha and the others became apparent. For the other Immigrants, this was a win—the beginning of their participative society—for Martha, it was total capitulation.

I then posed a hypothetical decision point, one that had not occurred previously: Decision 8: Once the negotiations were underway, should we continue or break off? The data were as follows:

Table 48.3   Decision 8

	MARTHA	TIM	ROGER	GERRI	BOB	NANCY	HANK	ANDY
RESIST	10	0	0	0	0	0	0	0
COOPERATE	0	10	10	10	10	10	10	10

Now the split was complete: Martha was ignored, her complaints were treated as misguided and irrelevant, her actions and emotions were viewed as eccentric. Whenever she spoke, there was little or no response. The "We" maintained its integrity—"We're all right . . . except for this Village Idiot."

A Mutant Moment

There was an explosion of energy in the room. Martha's depression was gone; she was her old voluble, enthusiastic self. Nothing about the societal outcome had changed: Martha had still lost; the Immigrants had not totally transformed the system as she had hoped. All that had happened was "seeing." But what a difference "seeing" made for Martha and the other Immigrants. This was a "seeing" not about a person but about a system—about the processes of the whole and how these processes affected the experiences of all members. But this was not just about Martha. Something happened in the room that I still do not fully understand and can only speculate about.

The explosion of energy was not limited to the Immigrants. The Elite and Managers had been observing this process for over two hours, and when the light went on for Martha and the Immigrants, it also went on for everyone in the room. People erupted into spontaneous applause. Conversations broke out that lasted deep into the night. I suspect that this was one of those rarest of human moments—a "Mutant Moment" that illuminates a new possibility in which each of us "swimmers" see the Swim itself and how the nature of the Swim has shaped our consciousness. In that moment of "seeing," we were fully conscious and free.

At one point in the conversation, Gerri, who had been Martha's most virulent adversary, said: "It could have been me."

"How do you mean?"

"Say I was the one who thought we should negotiate and everyone else said 'No.' I could easily have become the Village Idiot."

Exactly.

■

Who among us is incapable of seeing these dynamics of the "We"? When the "We" is for war, and the One Who Disagrees is for peace? Or the other way around? When the "We" has one view of appropriate sexuality, and the One Who Disagrees has another? When the "We" has one view of appropriate behavior or manner or dress, and the Ones Who Disagree have other views?

■

He: It seems to me I've seen these same things happen in Top groups.

She: That's right. The determining factor is not where you are in the hierarchy, but what the environmental conditions of your system are. In this case, the environment is one of shared vulnerability, that is, the feeling that something precious to your group is threatened: Its belief system or its way of life or its very survival.

He: So Top Executives who are feeling under attack from labor also get triggered into the "We," even though they're Tops. And they might have their Village Idiots who disagree with the "We."

She: Exactly. And when the Dominant group in society feels challenged by the Dominated, the Dominants get triggered into the "We."

He: So then it's "We" against "We."

She: Yes, and let me make this a bit more complex for you. Say there you are walking down the street when, suddenly, coming toward you is an odd looking sight: A barefoot person with spiked rows of hair alternating orange and purple, one ring in the nose, and six tinier rings penetrating her eyebrows. Your reaction?

He: I might laugh . . . or be shocked.

She: Maybe repulsed?

He: Maybe repulsed.

She: Because?

He: I think I see what you're getting at. I laugh or am shocked or repulsed because that's not the way "We" dress.

She: Exactly. And "We" don't see ourselves as conforming. "We" just see ourselves living.

■

There was one other consideration in the Martha case. Were those two Bottom group orientations really incompatible? Was it true that the group's choice was to pursue one or the other—*either* Martha's vision of total system transformation *or* the other members' more moderate aspirations for greater involvement and participation? It is a common illusion of the Bottom Space that divergencies cannot be tolerated, that they will destroy the "We." ("In unity there is strength.") But it is possible that there is another kind of strength, one that comes from the realization that many such divergencies are, in fact, creatively compatible; that working together in partnership, they can yield outcomes richer and more widely satisfying than those resulting from the pursuit of one *or* the other.

49 Where Is Everyone? A Mutant Bottom Group

We were in the middle of an organization exercise. There were twelve Bottom groups with five or six Workers in each. I was standing in the middle of the ballroom watching the action unfold when my eye was drawn to one particular Bottom group. *There was only one person sitting at this table.* I watched to see if the others had taken a break and would return shortly. But no, the table remained empty except for this one person. What happened here? Had the others quit the organization? Worse still, I wondered if they had dropped out of the exercise. I was feeling badly for this sole survivor. I walked over full of sympathy for his isolated condition only to find that something quite different was going on here, something I had never seen before.

He told me that there were several issues the group was facing. They hadn't been paid for several days; their manager had been tied up in meetings with Tops; there had been talk about potential bonuses for Workers; there were Customers complaining about not having their projects worked on; and there was interest in having a coffee break.

I wish I had been privy to the conversation among the group members, but I was not. The outcome, however, was the breakthrough idea that *all of these issues could be addressed simultaneously.*

"Our project is simple enough for me to handle alone," said the lone Worker, "and the others are out there seeing what they can do." Two members were hunting up disgruntled Customers to see if they could service them. One member was searching out their Manager to see if progress could be made both on collecting their overdue salaries and on exploring bonus possibilities for taking on additional Customer projects. And one member was bringing back coffee and pastries for a "working break."

This group had astounding success. They completed three projects: Customers were pleased; Workers got their pay along with healthy bonuses; the group enjoyed their "working break"; and they had an incredible sense of teamwork and accomplishment.

This is not how it normally goes in the Bottom group. Differentiation does not come naturally, even when differentiation is what is required for the system to successfully cope and prospect. The strong pressure to remain an integrated "We" works against needed differentiation.

More often you would find Bottom groups focused *either* on the work *or* on the working conditions, but not on both. There would be the "good Worker groups" just pouring their energies into the work ("We didn't even think about money," they would say righteously), only to find themselves unfairly underpaid at the end. Or there would be the "troublemaking Worker groups," so focused on issues of pay and working conditions that little or no work gets done.

And within these groups there would be tensions. Within the "good Worker group," there would be the submerged, disgruntled member who feels the group is being taken advantage of. Within the "troublemakers," there would be the submerged, disgruntled member who feels the group should be cooperating.

But here we had a breakthrough: We can work *and* we can make sure we are being treated fairly; we can produce *and* we can protect ourselves. From the outside this seem so obvious; on the inside, however, when we are in the grips of "We"-ness (when we are stuck on integration), we are often blind to the obvious.

50 Power Is Managing Differentiation

Once you see systems as wholes, you also begin to see power differently. From a systems perspective, power has little to do with strength or command presence or toughness or the position you hold or even the size and quality of the resources you control. *System Power is the ability to influence system processes*—to act in ways that enhance the capacity of the system to survive and develop in its environment, to cope with the dangers facing it and prospect among the opportunities. (Unless, of course, your goal is to destroy the system; then power becomes the ability to act in ways that reduce the system's capacity to survive and develop.) But to influence system processes you must first see them.

Mutant Bottom Groups

Fritz Steele was my colleague in the early Power Labs. Both of us were fascinated with differentiation. We were particularly struck by the inability of Bottom groups to deal with differentiation. Time after time we would see the following scenario unfold: A powerful "We" almost instantaneously develops as soon as the Bottoms find one another. The language quickly becomes one of "We" rather than "I." There is an openhanded sharing of resources and information; there is a sense of the specialness of the group along with negative evaluations of all others ("humorously" hostile gibes aimed at the Elite and Managers). There is a palpable protective boundary around the group; there is a strong tendency to strategize and make decisions together. Unspoken norms develop regarding acceptable limits of behavior, and there is little or no individual action beyond those limits. Then the endless, and often painful, meetings begin. They start with high enthusiasm—ideas fly regarding possible action steps—but then energy runs down as the meetings drag on and on and on. Nothing can be decided. The differentiations emerge:

"Let's go on strike."

"It's too soon for that."

"Let's try to work the system."

"We're just being sucked in."

"The Elite seem reasonable."

"They're patronizing us."

"I'm happy to go on working."

"I'm not."

The "We" struggles for agreement ("If only I could make my position clearer, you would agree"), but agreement never comes. And soon the same patterns of arguments repeat themselves, and frustration and depression set in. [As we have seen in the previous case, sometimes this process is avoided by submerging one side of the conflict into invisibility and subsequent Village Idiocy.]

A Remarkable Transformation of Energy

In the early days of the Power Lab, we staff were inventing our roles as we went along, just as we were inventing the Lab. Sometimes we would be full-fledged players in one part of the system or another; at other times, we were nonintervening observers; at other times, we were rarely intervening kibitzers; and sometimes, we were "Resource Persons." In one program, Fritz was the designated Resource Person, which meant that he was available to all parts of the system. One afternoon Fritz found himself in the middle of one of those downward spiraling Bottom group discussions—*"Let's go this way." "No, let's go that way." "Let me explain why this way is the way to go." "Let me try once again to show you how wrongheaded you are."* And on and on. Fritz stopped the conversation and said, with some enthusiasm, "It seems to me we have two teams here." And he made it sound as if these two teams were not competitors with one another but two units of the *same* team. "Why don't we see who is on which team?" And so the group began to divide. It was as if a jeweler had struck a diamond perfectly. Some members went quickly to one side or the other; they knew just where they stood. Others were more hard-pressed to choose; but in time, they all did. And then both groups went to work with this incredible release of creative energy. This transformation of energy was remarkable. What had seemed dead was now alive and cooking. What had seemed to be irreconcilable strategies now emerged as wholly compatible and complementary elements of one superstrategy. One group worked on constructing the new society—its constitution, judicial system, and so forth—while the other worked on strategies for "getting the Elite's attention."

To us this instantaneous transformation seemed like a miracle— from dead to alive, from mutual blocking to mutual enhancement. And when we reviewed the process with participants, it was only with difficulty that they remembered Fritz's role in this. It all seemed so natural as if it came out of them. *This was power*— influencing system energy.

What is striking about this is how in the Bottom Space differentiations that are not irreconcilable are experienced as such. This is the illusion of the Bottom Space. Under the pressure of maintaining the integrity of the "We," differences that could coexist become enemies to one another. Great power comes to us when we recognize and move past the illusion; and great destruction often follows when we do not. Consider the splintering that happens within labor, among revolutionary groups, within religions.

■

Many years ago I was conducting a seminar for Christian military chaplains. Throughout the seminar, there was considerable tension between certain liberal and conservative chaplains. At one point, one chaplain said to another in frustration, "At least we can agree that we are brothers in Christ." And he stretched out his hand toward the other. But his hand just hung there in the air.

51 Creating Powerful Bottom Groups

*In the Bottom group
special attention needs to be paid to
individuation and differentiation.
In the environment of shared vulnerability,
individuation and differentiation will not come naturally;
they have to be worked at
rigorously.*

1. Encourage individuation. In the Bottom group it is easy to hide in the "We"—to stand back and not put oneself at risk. Find out what different members bring to the party: What are their unique backgrounds, experiences, interests and skills? Encourage members to step forward and use (risk) their uniqueness in the service of the group's mission.

2. Encourage differentiation. Develop simultaneous multiple strategies for pursuing your mission. If strategies appear contradictory, look more deeply. It is often an illusion of the Bottom Space that differences appear to be incompatible when they are not.

3. Integrate regularly. As you become more individuated and differentiated, the need for regular integration will increase. Meet regularly; share your experiences; coach one another on your various strategies.

4. Bottom groups are prone to function under the banner: In Unity There Is Strength. A more powerful motto is: In Diversity There Is Strength. Your challenge in the Bottom group is to surface both the diversity of your members and the diversity of your strategies and to integrate these diversities in the service of your system's mission.

The Politics of Process

All organic systems—from the split-leaf philodendron to the common earthworm to General Motors— engage in similar system processes. They individuate, integrate, differentiate, and dedifferentiate. What distinguishes human systems from all other organic systems is that we think about these processes, we believe in them, we attach values to them, we politicize them, we favor one over the other.

52 Huddlers and Humanists

Sometimes
we *like* huddling—
thinking together,
planning together,
deciding together.
And sometimes
we *believe in* huddling.
Together
is the way we *should*
think,
plan,
decide
everything.

And so
we sit in our room
together
thinking,
planning,
deciding
everything.
An issue comes up.
Together
we think,
we plan,
we decide.
Another issue comes up
(there are three more at the door).
Together
we think,
we plan,
we decide.

Four new issues at the door,
six outside the window,
three opportunities just flew past
(waving bye-bye).

The issues flow in
under the door,
through the keyholes,
over the airwaves.
Our thinking grows fuzzy,
but still they come;
our planning is . . .
(What *happened* to planning?),

and still they come.
More issues:
Didn't we already handle that one?
Our decisions are random
(Someone has to decide).
At least we're still together
thinking
(barely),
planning
(We'll get back to that),
deciding.

One of us rises,
goes to the window,
spies three golden opportunities flying by—
juicy opportunities—
so close, so close.
("Should one of us look into this?" he ventures.)
Should *one*?
Together
they think,
they plan,
they decide,
as the golden opportunities
fly lazily by
(bye-bye)
and six more issues
slide under the door.

Well . . .
at least we're
together.

53 Amebocytes and Slugs: The Politics of Individuation and Integration

"Slime mold cells do it all the time . . . in each life cycle. At first they are single amebocytes swimming around, eating bacteria, aloof from each other, voting straight Republican. Then a bell sounds, and acrasin is released by special cells toward which the others converge in stellate ranks, touch, fuse together and construct the slug, solid as a trout. A splendid stalk is raised, with a fruiting body on top, and out of this comes the next generation of amebocytes, ready to swim across the same moist ground, solitary and ambitious."

Lewis Thomas, The Lives of a Cell[6]

■

He: Why are we talking about amebocytes and slugs?

She: Have you ever seen a more beautiful example?

He: Of what?

She: Individuation and integration. Isn't it beautiful?

He: I suppose it is.

She: Now let me ask you a question. What do you suppose would happen if the amebocytes decided to never come back?

He: I don't understand.

She: Say the amebocytes decided they never wanted to integrate again. They enjoy individuating. More than that, they believe in it. They want their freedom. They're against integration; they see it as constraining. So the amebocytes start carrying these placards saying: "Put an End to Big Government!" "Freedom Now!" "Deregulate the System!"

He: I don't see your point.

She: Or say the slug suddenly decides not to send out the next generation of amebocytes. The slug believes in integration. ("We're opposed to unrestrained individualism.") The slug is committed to the virtues of cooperation, loyalty, patriotism, connectedness.

He: Amebocytes and slugs don't think this way.

She: Maybe, maybe not. But who does think this way?

He: I think I'm getting the point.

She: I'm sure you are. We humans individuate and integrate. And we add a little extra to it. We attach values to these processes. We believe in them; they are the foundations of our organizations (or non-organizations); we build political parties; we form governments;we even go to war around these processes.

He: Are you saying that with us it's the Slugs against the Amebocytes?

She: That's a nice way of putting it.

The Slugs Versus the Amebocytes

Slug Systems

- The system comes first
- Loyalty, patriotism
- Align around the system's mission
- Amebocytes are selfish
- Amebocytes produce chaos
- Amebocytes will destroy our system
- Amebocytes threaten traditional values
- We must bring the Amebocytes into line or get rid of them
- Competition alienates Amebocytes from one another; it destroys their system

Amebocyte Systems

- The individual comes first
- Freedom
- Do your own thing
- Slugs are oppressive
- Slugs stifle creativity
- A Slug system isn't worth living in
- Slugs cling to the past
- We must get the Slugs off our backs

- Competition makes us great

He: So it's good against evil.

She: On whichever side you stand, there is an "evil empire" on the other.

She: If I asked you to match the following:

1. Male	a.	Individuation
2. Female	b.	Integration

What would you say?

He: I would say it would not be wise for us to get into this.

She: Good advice. Still, how would you match them?

He: (hesitantly) Well, the stereotype is Individuating Male, Integrating Female. The Hunter-Gatherer and the Maintainer-of-the-Campsite. But I'd prefer not to go much further with this.

She: Let us say, just for the purpose of discussion, that there is a consistent difference. Granting large areas of overlap and significant individual variation, let us say that males tend more toward individuation and females more toward integration.[7]

He: For the sake of discussion.

She: If there are differences, where is the problem? It's individuation and integration, it's Amebocyte and Slug—two indispensable system survival processes.

He: But that's not the way we talk about it.

She: Because we politicize the processes. Depending on where you stand, individuation and integration are either valued processes or disvalued ones.

Individuating Males	Integrating Females
■ Independent	■ Connecting
■ Strong	■ Nurturing
■ We do what needs to be done: The assertive actions	■ We do what needs to be done: The maintenance actions
■ Integrating females constrain us	■ Individuating males abandon us
■ We are rational, independent, objective	■ You are cold, detached, unfeeling
■ You avoid conflict	■ We preserve intimacy
■ You don't speak your mind	■ You dominate the conversation
■ Male individuation is what made our country great	■ Male individuation is what led to colonialism, imperialism, the oppression of women, people of color, native Americans

She: So long as we politicize individuation and integration, it's impossible to create systems that recognize the contributions and limitations of *both* processes.

55 Or Would You Rather Be an Earthworm?

The earthworm
is a simple/generalized system—
little differentiation,
much dedifferentiation.
The human organism
is a complex/specialized system—

much differentiation,
little dedifferentiation.

Cut off the human head,
and we're dead.
Cut off the head of the earthworm,
and it grows a new head.

■

He: First Amebocytes and Slugs, now earthworms. What are you up to?

She: Differentiation and dedifferentiation. These are two fascinating
     processes. Differentiation is about endless possibilities—system parts
     specializing, becoming increasingly different from one another.

He: And dedifferentiation?

She: Dedifferentiation is about redundancy, commonality, replaceability.
     It's about system parts remaining similar to one another.

He: So?

She: These are two different strategies for system survival. One says:
     "Let's develop as great a variety among our parts as we can—even
     if our parts lose their commonality." The other says: "Let's main-
     tain the replaceability of our parts even at the cost of variety."

He: I think I follow this, but what has this got to do with social sys-
     tems . . . society . . . the *BIG* issues?

She: Most systems place their bets for survival on one process or the
     other. The earthworm is betting on dedifferentiation at the
     expense of differentiation: Keep it simple, keep the parts replace-
     able. The earthworm is doing pretty well with its bet; it's been
     around for a lot longer than humans have.

     The human organism has put its money on differentiation at the
     expense of dedifferentiation—the body has an incredibly rich array
     of tools for interacting with the environment. The downside is our
     bodies are extremely vulnerable to the loss of key parts.

He: (impatiently): And so?

She: Dedifferentiation without differentiation can be quite boring—like
     the earthworm.

He: I see that.

She: And differentiation without dedifferentiation can be quite deadly.

He: And?

She: And that is what is happening to this single system called Humanity.

56 Differentiation, Inquiry, Warfare

From the outside,
differentiation is beautiful;
from the inside,
it is warfare.

From the outside,
it is open-ended inquiry;
from the inside,
it is fixed and final truths.

From the outside,
it is "Let us explore all of the possibilities for this system."
From the inside,
it is "Let us pursue my way, the right way, the only
True Way."

From the outside,
all possibilities seem worth exploring;
from the inside,
your possibility threatens the validity of my possibility.

From the outside,
there is an inevitability and beauty in our differentiations;
from the inside,
there is pain and loss—
separation and divorce,
the dissolution of partnerships,
costly reorganizations,
abuse and oppression,
holy wars,
ethnic conflicts,
holocausts.

Are you telling me that the Truth is
one religion
or the other?
Are you telling me that the Truth is
one sexual orientation
or the other?
Are you telling me that the Truth is
big family or small
or none at all?
Expand or stand pat?
Black or white?
Fast or slow?
Your country or mine?
Now or later?
Hit 'em hard or be reasonable?
Your race or mine?

Such Truth exists on the inside;
from the outside
it's all inquiry.

He: You're treading on some dangerous ground here.

She: How is that?

He: You are diminishing everything we hold precious—my neighborhood, my country, . . . my religion!

She: And how do I do that?

He: To you they are all options . . . possibilities . . . explorations. It could be this, . . . but then again it could be that. You take away the specialness. . . . My country right or wrong. You take away the possibility of belief. You call my religion a spiritual quest as if it's merely an option . . . one of several possibilities.

She: Isn't it that?

He: What if I think differently? What if I believe that it is the One True Religion?

She: Yes?

He: Well then, where will dedifferentiation take me? If I ask myself what can be learned from exploring other spiritual quests, won't that change how I experience my religion?

She: I would hope so.

He: You would hope so!

She: I would hope so.

He: But won't it ruin it for me? I could never have the faith that I have now.

She: Maybe yes, maybe no. Who knows what you might discover? Maybe you would have a much deeper and richer faith than you have now. Does that ruin it? Or transform it?

He: Transform it?

She: From an answer to a continuing exploration. It is a big question after all. Transformation involves taking your quest to another level. There will be loss of the old certainties, but the new place may be a much more powerful one for you.

He: I feel the old dance shaking, and I don't know if I can handle this one.

She: It's your choice. It's always your choice.

An Ode to Dedifferentiation

Differentiation yields national identity and pride;
and without dedifferentiation,
it yields International Warfare.
Differentiation yields
richly varied religious expressions;
and without dedifferentiation,
it yields Holy Wars.
Differentiation yields
ethnicity;
and without dedifferentiation,
it yields Holocausts
and Ethnic Cleansing.
Differentiation results in
power differences;
and without dedifferentiation,
it results in the Dominant and the Dominated.
Differentiation yields
a variety of sexual orientations;
and without dedifferentiation,
it yields Sexual Oppression.

Seeing involves
seeing what is
and seeing what is missing.
Wherever there is Differentiation,
we would do well to attend to Dedifferentiation.
As we elaborate our differences,
we also need to develop and maintain our commonality.

58 Systems: Passive, Political, or Robust

When we are blind to system processes,
we fall into them—
passively and reflexively;
we fall into differentiation
and get stuck there;
we fall into individuation
and get stuck there;
we fall into integration
and get stuck there.

When we are blind to system processes,
we politicize them—
we value certain processes
and disvalue others:
It's individuation or integration,
differentiation or dedifferentiation.

When we see system processes,
we can choose:
We can choose to create robust human systems:
we can chose to pursue all system processes
purposefully and zestfully,
to individuate
and to integrate,
to differentiate
and to dedifferentiate,
because each process
enhances our system's capacity
to survive and develop in its environment,
to cope with the dangers it faces
and prospect among the opportunities.

Individuation

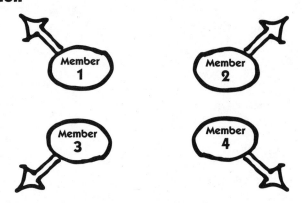

Four system members individuating.

The zestful pursuit of Individuation provides the system with diversity.

It is through zestful Individuation that system members develop their unique capacities—their special knowledge, skills, abilities, and interests. These unique capacities then become their potential contributions to the system. In the Robust System, members do not hide in the "We"; they continue to develop their individuality—to learn, to grow, to stretch, to be on the outer edge of their possibilities as human beings.

In the Robust System, members encourage and support one another in the zestful elaboration of their unique interests, passions, and abilities.

Integration

The zestful pursuit of Integration gives the system coordinated movement in the service of some larger function, purpose, or mission.

The Robust System has a powerful mission of its own, a mission that is separate from the individual missions of its members and beyond what system members could accomplish alone.

In the Robust System, members are committed to the system's mission. They value that mission and derive deep personal satisfaction from being a part of it and contributing to it.

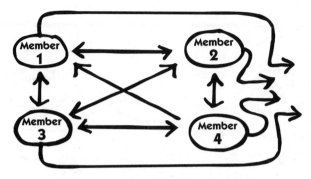

Four system members integrating.

In the Robust System, members function in a coordinated manner—enhancing one another's performance through providing one another information and resources—and members modulate their own behaviors in the service of the whole.

Differentiation

A system differentiating, pursuing strategies A-F

The zestful pursuit of Differentiation gives the system complexity.

Through Differentiation the system develops multiple mechanisms and processes for coping with the dangers and prospecting among the opportunities in its environment. Differentiation enables the system to interact complexly with its environment (generating a variety of approaches for achieving the same goal), and it enables the system to deal with many different dangers and opportunities in its environment.

Dedifferentiation

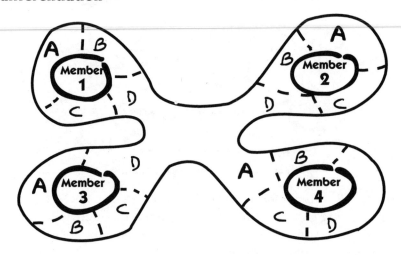

A dedifferentiated system.
The system has four capacities (A, B, C, and D).
Each of the system members (1, 2, 3, and 4) is capable
of performing all four system functions.

The zestful pursuit of Dedifferentiation gives the system parts commonality, mutual understanding, and replaceability.

In the Dedifferentiated state, whatever capacity the system has is widely spread throughout the system. In the Dedifferentiated state, there is a high degree of mutual understanding throughout the system: Members are knowledgeable about one another's functions; members are, to varying degrees, interchangeable; members are empowered in the sense that each member is capable of performing a wide range of system functions; and the system as a whole is less vulnerable to the loss of any member because members are more interchangeable.

■

He: So let me see if I have this. Any system can be a Robust System—whether you're talking about the entire system, or the Top, Middle, or Bottom systems within the larger system. They're all candidates.

She: Right.

He: The trick is to be aware of what is happening to your system . . .

She: . . . and what is not happening.

He: To not let yourself get stuck on one process or the other.

She: Right.

He: To zestfully pursue Individuation, Integration, Differentiation and Dedifferentiation.

She: Right.

He: To not be driven by the environment.

She: Right.

He: And to not be driven by your beliefs and values.

She: Right.

He: I think I've got it.

 # The Dance of the Robust System: Ballet Notes

Summary

The troupe enters the dance hall. They are the prototypical human system; they are the family, the work group, the team, the organization, the nation. They are in search of a mode of existence for themselves. What kind of human system shall we be? There are at least six members in the troupe—three pairs or, depending on the size of the production, there could be many more. In Act I their search takes them to unsuccessful experiences; first with Anarchy, then Totalitarianism, and finally Democracy. In Act II they succeed in creating the Robust System. The Robust System develops in four integrated dances—the Mission, Differentiation, Dedifferentiation, and in the wild climax, the three dances are woven together into the Dance of Robust Systems.

Act I   The Search

Anarchy: The Dance of Individuality

Each member is doing his and her own dance. There is liberty, freedom. The variety of dances is great. Each is beautiful in its own right yet the overall effect is disconcerting. In time, chaos develops; the dances begin to interfere with one another. Dancers bump into one another. Conflicts and fights develop. Members pulling at one another. Withdrawing. Sulking. Dancers fight with one another for space for their individual dances. Collisions increase. Frustration. Warfare. In the end, the dancers collide and collapse in a heap.

Totalitarianism: The Dance of Uniformity

Members are one unit, perfectly synchronized. Everything is neat and orderly, not a person is out of step. There are regimented marches, goose-stepping, June Taylor type configurations. This order is pleasing to the eye, especially following the chaos of the previous dance. Periodically a dancer breaks out of the pattern into an individual dance. These bursts of individuality are beautiful yet clearly out of place. They are quickly ridiculed, and the dancer is brought back into line. There is one exquisite individual performance that causes the others to stop and stare, first in admiration, then in anger. The exquisite dancer is finally shamed into conforming to the unit. The dance ends with all individuals brought back into line. There is a sadness to this.

Democracy: The Dance of Consensus

This is more of a debate about dance than a dance itself. Suggestions about which dance to engage in are discussed: Shall we dance this way or that? There is considerable enthusiasm at the outset over particular possibilities; this is soon followed by much deliberation, criticism, naysaying, suggested modifications, voting—all of which eventually drain the energy out of the dancers. Suggested dances become weaker, more tentative. Voting continues, apathy sets in. The dance ends in a vote; most dancers are by now so beaten down that they don't even vote.

Act II   The Robust System

There are a series of integrated dances all leading to the Dance of the Robust System.

The Dance of Mission

The dancers explore the question: What can we be? They face outward and explore their environment. What is out there? What is missing? What can we be in that environment? What can we create? What can we accomplish? What is our possibility? They face inward, exploring one another. How do we want to be with one another? There is an exploration and, in the end, a discovery of our mission—of who we will be both in the world and in relationship to one another. There is the exhilaration of possibility.

The Dance of Differentiation

Differences emerge among the dancers as to the best path to follow in order to fulfill their mission. There is a pull to go one way or the other. At first there is struggle; it will be this dance or that. Struggle yields to agreement to pursue this and that. Enthusiasm and release of energy. Simultaneously different dances emerge—the differentiated dances. These dances begin tentatively; they gradually develop in strength and beauty. In the end, we are treated to at least three very different and very beautiful dances going on simultaneously.

The Dances of Dedifferentiation

The three differentiated dances continue. Dancers begin to get curious about one another's dances. What are they doing over there? In the following dances, members come together; they learn about the others' dances, coach one another, and perform one another's dances.

Show. Each differentiated dance is brought to the center and performed while the others observe.

Coach. The dancers, in turn, coach one another on their dances and make suggestions as to how to strengthen each dance. There is an exuberance in both the giving and taking of coaching.

Dances of the whole. Each differentiated dance group comes to the center and performs its dance; they are then joined by all the others; everyone learns to do every dance. There is a series of exuberant dances of the whole.

The Dance of the Robust System

In the finale, all of the elements of the Robust System are recreated: There is a reexamination of the Mission; there are Differentiations, some old ones and some new; there are exuberant dances of the whole; and throughout, there are individual dances (previously suppressed dances are elaborated and honored). The ballet ends in an explosive burst of individuality and commonality, difference and oneness.

 # 61 A Remarkable, If Somewhat Premature, Epiphany

He: My God! I'm just beginning to see how big all of this is!

She: Tell me.

He: You've just unraveled a gigantic mystery. Don't you see it? There is all this pain in the world—divorce, broken relationships, alienation. And it's all so stupid. It just doesn't have to *be*. None of it. We're just victims. We let it happen to us. Just because we don't see. It's all so clear and logical.

She: So?

He: So you've explained it to me, and now I want to explain it to others, to the world!

She: And how do you propose to do that?

He: It's all so clear. You just have to explain it to people. Show them how it all works. Show them the dances. Draw the pictures.

She: And?

He: And they'll see the light. They'll stop. They'll see how stupid they've been. How unnecessary all the pain has been.

She: (with a hint of sarcasm) And that is just what people do best, isn't it? See how stupid they've been.

He: But it is all so clear! I've got the whole pattern. I'm ready to move. This is not deep. I have it all summarized on this card. I am ready to move out and make my fortune.

His Magic Consultant's Card

System	Pitfall	Need to Work On
Top	Over-Diff (Turf)	Int and Dediff
Middle	Over-Ind (Alienation)	Int (then Diff)
Bottom	Over-Int (GroupThink)	Ind and Diff

She: You may be right. For some people at least. There is some rationality in the world. You show them, and they'll see the light. A slap on the forehead. Aha! So that's the problem, and here's how to fix it—His Magic Consultant's Card.

He: Yes, and I am ready to move. I am going to alleviate a lot of pain in this world.

She: Yes, and I hope you do. But there is something you don't see.

He: Which is?

She: People are not just minds. They are not pure rationality. There is more at stake here than just seeing. People are emotional beings. They have investments in preserving the past and the present. They do not appreciate the possibility that they have been wrong. This is a very big deal. You must see that! What does it mean for me to have to accept the fact that my partnership did not have to fail, that my marriage did not have to fail, that these people I have such poor evaluations of might really be all right people, just like me. I have made investments in these feelings; I have justified

199

them to myself many, many times in the past. And you, with your Magic Consultant's Card, you think that I will let go of all of that. Just because it makes sense!

He: Then what?

She: Do exactly what you said. But don't give up after the first "No," or the second, or the third. The greater the investment in the past . . .

He: . . . the louder the sounds of the old dance shaking.

She: Exactly.

SUMMARY

In this section, we have explored the costs of process blindness. We have seen how, in our blindness, we are vulnerable to the tugs of our environment—how we get stuck on certain processes to the neglect of others; how we passively and reflexively fall into nonproductive and destructive patterns of interaction—Turf Warfare, Alienation, and GroupThink. We have also seen how, in our blindness to system processes, we politicize these processes, valuing some and disvaluing others; and we have seen how, in so doing, we limit the power of our systems. Finally we have explored the possibility of seeing system processes. When we see system processes, we can choose. We are driven neither by our system's environment nor by our politics. We can strive to create Robust Human Systems—systems in which we develop, respect, and encourage our individuality and our community, our diversity and our commonality.

Epilogue: The Next Act—Seeing More

She: Well, can you see systems now?

He: Yes, I am amazed at what I see. I'm aware of the stories I make up. I wonder about the history of events: *What led up to this moment?* I'm constantly seeing myself in relationship with others—as a Top or a Bottom, an End or a Middle, a Provider or a Customer. I'm more aware of Turf and Alienation and GroupThink. I see how processes get politicized. I see quite a bit.

She: You see the dances?

He: Oh yes, I see the dances. And I see that I can change the dances. And I see that that's not always easy, that there are plenty of opportunities to retreat into the old dances.

She: And resistance?

He: The sound of the old dance shaking.

She: Still, you seem puzzled.

He: I see quite a bit, yet I'm still struck by how much I *don't* see.

She: Ah, but that it such an important beginning! It leads you to question your experiences, and that is critical if we are to stop our misguided battles with one another.

He: I think I understand, but say more.

She: We are like Barth's "swimmers." We are in our own night-sea journey. We have our experiences and our explanations. We have our schools of philosophy. We are Burdened and we blame circumstances. We are Oppressed and we blame higher-ups. We are Torn and we blame our jobs. We are Alienated from others, or locked into territorial struggles with them, or caught up in fantasies of our group's superiority, feeling certain that our experiences of others and ourselves are grounded in reality. We dominate others, unaware that we are doing so. We hate others and oppress them, assured that our feelings and actions are justified. All of this happens because we do *not* question the validity of our experiences.

We do not see the swim we are in, we do not understand its meaning, nor do we see how our experiences are shaped by the form and function of that swim. Without that "seeing" we are at the mercy of the swim.

He: Yes, I understand that. But you said something else just now, something about the *meaning* of the swim. Until now we have not talked about meaning. Are you saying that you know the meaning of the swim we are in?

She: I think I do.

He: And?

She: It is a test.

He: Of what?

She: A test of our humanity. It is a test of our ability to move to a new level of possibility for ourselves as human beings. Blind reflex has taken a terrible toll; some of the damage has been minor, some catastrophic: Misunderstanding, hate, disappointment, lost opportunities, oppression, destruction. And we humans show no lack of capacity for continuing along that path.

And then there is this other path—more difficult to discern; we are unclear as to where it leads, hesitant to take the first step. And rightly so. That first step requires great humility. Maybe, in our system blindness, we have been wrong about these others; maybe, in sliding into one dance or the other, we have misjudged them. Maybe it was great folly for us to hate these others, fear them, separate ourselves from them, escape from them, avoid them, dominate them, hurt them, oppress them, destroy them. Maybe it was all a terrible mistake. And maybe we are still doing it.

So that is the test. To see systems or be blind to them. The costs of blindness are clear. Who knows what possibilities "seeing" holds for us?

He: That's all?

She: It's a beginning.

Notes

Act One

1 John Barth, "Night-Sea Journey" in *Lost in the Funhouse*. New York: Doubleday, 1968.

2 If you need to know what the night-sea journey is, call my office (617-437-1640), and I will tell you the meaning of the Swim. However, be forewarned, although I feel certain that my story is *the* story, it may be just another story.

3 *October Project*, Unpublished manuscript. Boston: Power & Systems, Inc., 1986.

Act Two

4 The Daniel case is taken from Barry Oshry, *In the Middle*. Boston: Power & Systems, Inc., 1994.

Act Three

5 The dynamics of Middle integration are discussed in greater detail in Barry Oshry, *In the Middle*. Boston: Power & Systems, Inc., 1994.

6 Lewis Thomas, *Lives of a Cell*. New York: Viking, 1974.

7 My point here is not to establish whether there are systematic male/female biases toward individuation or integration, but merely to explore the consequences of such differences, if they exist. I cite the possibility of systematic differences based on my reading of the following:

Carol Gilligan, *In a Different Voice*. Cambridge: Harvard University Press, 1982. Gilligan poses a distinct female orientation to morality, one that reflects the importance of what I would call integrative concerns—connection, interdependencies, caring, and responsibility.

Deborah Tannen, *In You Just Don't Understand*. New York: Random House, 1990. Tannen points to consistent differences in male/female communication patterns, differences that are consistent with individuating/integrating tendencies: Men, being more competitive, try to avoid being one-down; women, being inclined to preserve intimacy, avoid conflict.

Robert May, *Sex and Fantasy*. New York: W. W. Norton, 1980. May's research points to consistent gender differences, again consistent with individuation and integration: Males being more likely to function in detached, isolated fashion in solitary work. Rational, independent, and objective are words May uses to describe the positive side of the male tendency; he uses the words cold, detached, and unfeeling to describe the negative side. May writes, "Women have less of a penchant for deciding things independent of the relevant network of connections. . . . They put a faithfulness to human ties above dedication to 'principle' or pure 'independence' of judgment."

David Bakan, *The Duality of Human Existence*. Boston: Beacon Press, 1966. Bakan cites research demonstrating consistent male/female differences in "agency" (interchangeable with individuation) and "communion" (interchangeable with integration).

The Author

For over thirty years, Barry Oshry has been on a single-minded quest to unlock the mysteries of power and powerlessness in social system life. Throughout his career he has created organizational and societal simulations that have served both as learning environments for participants and research laboratories for himself. He began his work in the 1960s at Boston University, where he developed large-scale organizational simulations for undergraduates in business. Throughout the 1960s, Oshry continued his research at the University and at the National Training Laboratories' Management Work Conferences and Community Laboratories. In 1970, he created the Power & Systems Laboratory (now called the Power & Leadership Conference), and since the mid-1970s, he has developed and conducted organizational simulations—with Tops, Middles, Bottoms, and Customers—that have been used to create "system sight" in organizations and institutions throughout the world. In 1994, Oshry received a David L. Bradford Educator Award.

For better or worse, since creating the Power & Systems Laboratory, Oshry has insulated himself from the burgeoning organization and management literature. He has limited himself to what he sees directly, remaining "uncontaminated" (and also unenlightened) by the theoretical perspectives of others. Over the years, he has observed and participated in hundreds of organizational and societal exercises, listened to participants describe their experiences in these programs in other real-world organizational and institutional settings. It is through these many observations and conversations that a unique "Oshry" framework for seeing systems has developed. When asked where his theory comes from, Oshry quotes Elvis Presley, "I don't sound like anybody." He does admit, however, to having been strongly influenced by lateral reading in the physical and biological sciences.

In his writings, Oshry often deals with serious issues in nontraditional ways, "the dance" being one of his most prevalent metaphors. Oshry's essay, "The Terrible Dance of Power," and book, *The Dance of Disempowerment*, have been the bases of theatrical productions by the Seattle Public Theatre and the Seattle Mime Company, and there have been numerous dramatic readings of his works.

Oshry is married to Karen Ellis Oshry, who has been his partner and collaborator in all ventures for over twenty-five years—from waiting on tables to theory development to gourmet dining to conducting workshops around the world. Karen has been the first reader of all his writings. She is a sharp observer of systems, a tough critic, an empowering coach, a co-sufferer in the hard times, and a co-celebrant in the good ones. The Oshrys enjoy the friendship of two children, their spouses, and two grandchildren.

In 1975, the Oshrys founded Power & Systems, Inc., a not-for-profit educational corporation, whose staff continues to offer Power & Leadership Conferences, Organization Workshops, and programs on dominance and diversity for organizations and institutions around the globe.

Barry Oshry can be reached at:

Power & Systems, Inc.
P.O. Box 990288
Prudential Station
Boston, Massachusetts 02199-0288
Phone: 617-437-1640
Fax: 617-437-6713
Internet: BOSHRY18@aol.com